Death by Renaissance evokes and invokes a time that is gone and a place that is becoming unrecognizable. Powerful currents run through this book—anger, love for a community, commemoration of their way of life. Refusing to be too easily understood, the best of these poems demand and amply repay repeated reading.

—Michael Palma

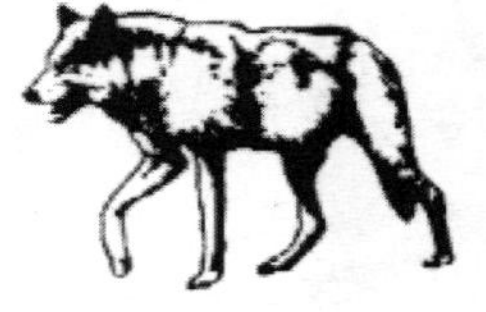

Death by Renaissance

Poems and Photos

Paola Corso

Working Lives Series
Bottom Dog Press
Huron, Ohio

Bottom Dog Press, Inc.
PO Box 425
Huron, Ohio 44839
http://members.aol.com/lsmithdog/bottomdog
Contact: Lsmithdog@aol.com

Cover and Book Design by Larry Smith
Cover Photos:
(front) author Paola Corso and sister Mary Ann (1958)
(back) George Thomas Mendel

Archival photos courtesy of
The Corso & Calderone families and
The Allegheny-Kiski Valley Historical Society

Acknowledgments on page 99

Special Thanks for the contiued support of
The Ohio Arts Council

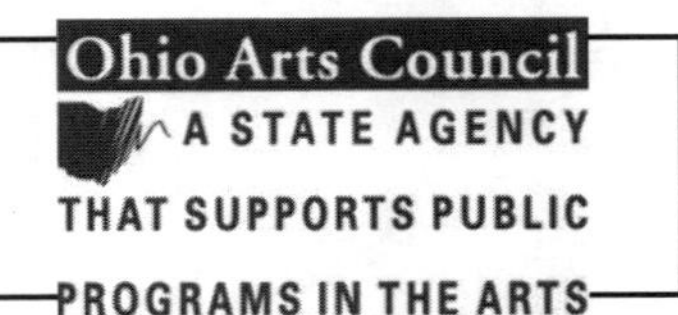

Contents

For my sister and my mother,
in memory of my father,
Mariano Procopio "Mario P." Corso (1925-2002)

and for Michael and Giona

Author's Preface

The Corso in me had to ask my father when he was dying of cancer about his course in life, his way to salvation. He told me it was a walk along the river, past the school where he dago flunked until he learned the speak, the steel mill where he operated a sweatbox crane, then to war to gun a fighter plane. The university to skin a couple of degrees only to go home again. To the office where he showed his old teachers this dago had learned how to write his name when he signed their paychecks. A 76-year-old man who was determined to lick his cancer and get back to work.

I revisit my father's course and the course of his river town, the treatments he endured to try to prolong his life and the development schemes from gambling to prisons to chain-store malls to tourism to jumpstart dying economies not just in the Pittsburgh area but all across the country. I wonder how these blue-collar towns can be revived so that the community purpose on which they were founded and the history that once gave them life aren't laid to rest in the process. Not that I want to romanticize Pittsburgh's steel industry. I simply employ "the power of memory and the poetics of witness," to quote working-class studies author Janet Zandy. I write as one who left, for those like my sister who stayed.

I navigate the course of development and its consequences in Pittsburgh river towns, particularly the human toll exacted on a vanishing blue-collar class and the environmental degradation from industry. Can what was done be undone? Is there a recourse? I turn to river imagery throughout the book because the river is Pittsburgh's sanguine gift of motion. It moved me to write this book in a current. The flow was its own, not mine.

But the facts are ours: a city in the early '80s where the manufacturing sector lost nearly 80,000 jobs, and the suicide rate was twice the national average. Divorces were up. So was domestic violence. Unemployment and underemployment were at 20 percent. Pittsburghers who never ventured beyond their corner bar left family behind to find work in other parts of the country. It was as if someone pried open their mouths, reached down their throats as they swallowed the same fish they had been eating for generations and yanked it out. And unlike the legendary man of steel, Joe Magarac, who was such a devoted mill Hunk that he melted himself down in the furnace to sacrifice himself to the steel industry, most workers didn't jump into the fire. They were thrown from production line to soup kitchen line because they never made the transition to the high-tech industry.

Pittsburgh's rivers ranked among the most polluted in the country, its industrial waste dumps among the most toxic. One was in my backyard in the woods along the river where I swam, the trees where I hid behind to play strip poker. They were leveled and suddenly I was naked.

Perhaps it's easy for me to ask these questions because I no longer live in Pittsburgh and I pose them in the safe haven of poetry where I'm only vulnerable as a writer—not like the Pittsburghers who have no work clothes to wear. Yet every time I visited my dying father, I agonized over having to leave him. Now I have the same ambivalence over his dying river town. Is my course its recourse? Will I get a second chance to give it new life and it me? I write about what it would be like to swim in my cove again, rocked and swaddled, brown at the edge of green. My head bobs the eyeful water, light enough to begin again.

Brooklyn, NY, November 2003

THE SAME FISH TWICE

1.

Renascence,

what naval sky we follow to eye
the forest, what corded sound we murmur to ax
the trees, how warmly we dress in lining unbroken
to log the timbered cabin, to unpack the covered wagon,
why we suck our thumbs while reaching inside,
pulling the pail to fish the river, to fry the trout;

(baby, baby, you're out).

2.

Progress,

what it weighs when we set it on the plate
to feed our neighbor, what it pays to lick it *clean*,
bones thrown in fiery steel, how much to ash the beam,
how high we count on our fingers and toes to span the bridge
for walking, how far across yet miss the inevitable stop,

strides beyond,

limping back,
wind beating inside our ear through cleft mats of hair
and blowing holes through our underwear.

3.

Appearance,

what polka-dotted line we sign to open
our neighbor's mouth, just how to unswallow the neighborly
fish, what apron to wear to unfry the trouted dish
to pail it back into the river, to repack the wagon
before razing the cabin, digging, digging below
puddles of lace to plant the log, to thicken the forest

(too dark to grow, too much to weed.)

For One Who Leaves

SATURDAY MORNINGS

Truth is I resented my weekly chore of
> dusting
>> mill soot under my dresser doily,

on the windowsill, baseboard, and floor,
> beneath
>> the corners of my desk blotter, using spit

and four-letter words with each glide over black specks
> so fine
>> I couldn't tell how dirty the surface was

until it soiled my white rag, an old T-shirt
> my mother
>> cut and folded into handy squares

she made the size of a loaf of bread
> for a family
>> of four or six or eight depending.

I would rather have left the house,
> gone
>> to the movies, a football game,

gone shopping for a tighter pair of jeans or
> darker
>> shade of nail polish.

Truth is my mother couldn't have cared
> less
>> that I hated having to clean my room

every Saturday; she was grateful because dust meant
> jobs
>> in an industry where the blacker the better,

angel's dust she called it but how could that be,
                    angel's
            dust, the color of the devil.

MY VERY OWN CLEANING LADY

I always thought I'd do my own cleaning,
                never
          forget the working-class way

of Italian American women like my mother who kept
                a broom
          beside her front door as if it were

a sign that read, "We work hard, we clean hard
                so wipe
          your damn feet on the welcome mat before

you step inside." The broom was a sign that well-off
                'mericans
          didn't understand; they saw it as clutter

that belonged in a tool shed behind a fence
                in the back
          yard with the snow blower and the leaf blower

and the lawn mower. Then I moved to Brooklyn,
                bought
          a co-op apartment, had a baby and a contractor who

skipped town in the middle of renovation. He left me in
                dirty
          living hell with a nursing newborn,

650 square feet of filth and six ounces of breast milk
                every four hours,
          dust he knew my own prosperity created

because I could afford to add on a second bedroom. I was
                another
          'merican in this immigrant's eyes who'd just pay

to have someone else clean up after him. It was
        all I could
     do to take a shower but I ignored signs

in our lobby that advertised "PhDs who clean." It wasn't
        in me
     to hire someone, even a scholar gathering

dust samples for a doctoral thesis. I still thought
        money
     would never change hands to get the apartment

clean when my mother came for a visit. She wanted to but
        didn't ask
     why not a house in Pittsburgh, why I waited so long

to leave my job and have a baby. She filled a bucket
        of water,
     scrubbed the floor on her knees one square foot

at a time. Payback for all those Saturday mornings. As she
        rinsed
     her rag and said the contractor's name in vain,

I rested on the sofa with my son, remembering
        dust to dust.

MY ITALIAN GRANDMOTHER'S ADVICE
WHEN I LEFT PITTSBURGH FOR NEW YORK CITY

If you fly, land in LaGuardia Airport.

If you drive, take the Verrazano Bridge.

If you get lost, turn on Frank Sinatra Highway.

If you have to stop for gas, fill up in Little Italy.

If you're hungry for candy, buy a Joe DiMaggio bar.

If your car breaks down, tow it to Lee Iacocca at the Chrysler Building.

If you rent an apartment, live next door to Seinfeld's friend, Giorgio Costanz.

If you vote in the next election, write in Geraldine Ferraro.

If you go to the theater, attend Tony and Tina's Wedding.

If you can't find a job, see Mario Cuomo.

If you still can't find a job, use the 100 lire I gave you and come home.

EXPRESSED

My father drove 382 miles from Pittsburgh to Brooklyn and didn't find a parking space. His welcoming was a $60 ticket and sticky sap all over his windshield from the sycamores on our tree-lined street. We moved the car to a legal spot then took a taxi to Home Depot to buy light fixtures and to Home Depot again for a toilet seat because I couldn't leave a nursing baby for longer than a few hours at a time.   After my father hung the ceiling light, he picked up operating instructions for a Purely Yours breast pump. I sat at the kitchen table with my nursing bra flaps down, exposing breasts hard and engorged while he rigged tubing to the machine, set the dial, and handed me the suction cup. When my milk began to sputter into the bottle, he winked and left me with a pitcher of water to drink as I expressed one breast at a time in calibrated dribs and drabs. The room grew dark, but he came back to switch on the ceiling fixture he had just installed. And in his light, my eyes gradually began to adjust to the bold pattern of the newly hung wallpaper, to the full bottle of milk in front of me, waiting to see my cream rise to the top in the freezer before the faint tint of blue.

THE DOCTOR MAKES HIS DIAGNOSIS *

I have two cities but only one home

that is my mother's womb
with one long umbilical cord
that reaches across thousands
of frequent flyer miles.

I have two apartments and one window

filled with pleats of light
and a sooty curtain
that no matter the color
is a checkered gray.

I have "an abiding devotion" to my birthplace,

so when I go back to Pittsburgh,
I'm *stupida* for living in Brooklyn
and when I'm living in Brooklyn,
I'm mad with longing.

I have an "afflicted imagination"

that incapacitates my body, causing
nausea, loss of appetite, high fever,
pathological changes in the lungs,
brain inflammation, and cardiac arrest.

I have a "lifeless and haggard countenance,"

an "idleness conducive to daydreaming"
about thick village milk and Iron City beer,
about the sounds of bagpipes and Terrible Towels
whipping in stadium winds.

I have three college degrees and seven bookcases

but rely solely on "associationist magic."
When I climb the stairs to the torch
of the Statue of Liberty, I imagine being
at the top of an idle factory smokestack.

I have a "highly contagious disease" but curable

if you purge my stomach, induce torture and pain.
I can be ridiculed, laughed out of my homesickness
unless you see me as a working-class woman
who does a white-collar job with blue-collar hands.

[Swiss Doctor Johannes Hofer coined the word "nostalgia"
in his 1688 medical dissertation *Dissertatio Medica de Nostalgia.*]

I'LL LOOK UP AT THE CEILING OF HEINZ CHAPEL
AND SEE A PAINTING OF MY LAST JUDGMENT

Will opium or leech cure my diseased bone,
my gut rumbling under the influence.
Will a trip home allow me to atone
in three rivers stinking with effluence.
As I float there, will nymphs of the fountain
lead me to pray at their golden altar
or let me drift upstream to be counted
amongst the believers if I enter.
But no one will know me when I return
unless I choose their vision and reverse
to a time before the fission of a job force:
households without expense or loss, a town
where steel doesn't bend, a chapel fresco
uncracked, a Sistine finger that lets go.

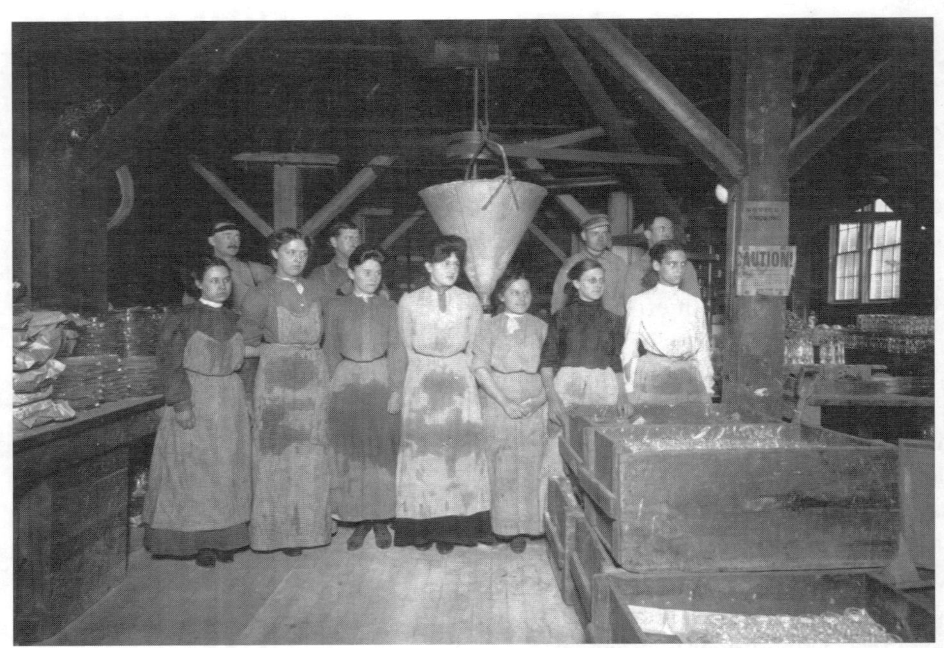

Glass workers in Allegheny-Kiski Valley (c. 1890)

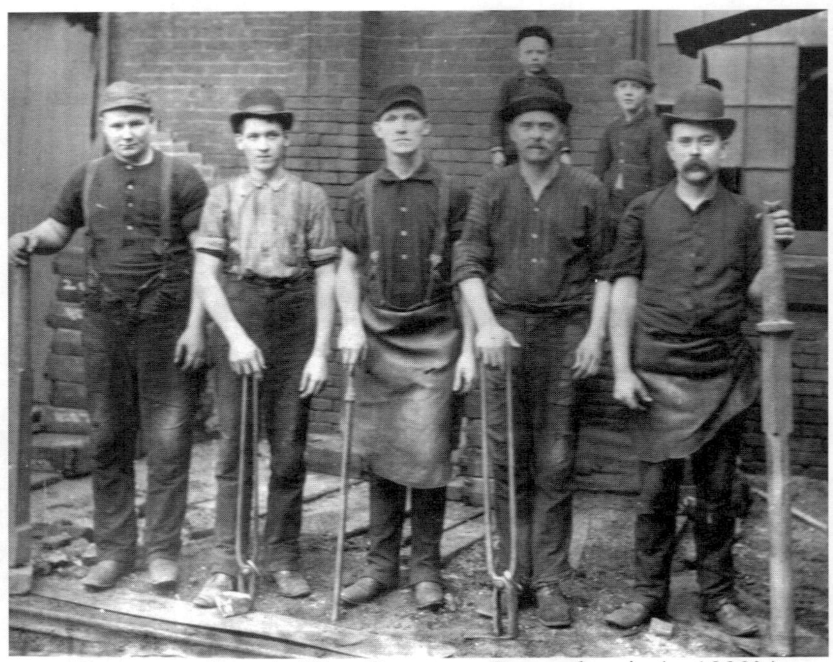

Bronze workers in West Tarentum, Pennsylvania (c. 1890's)

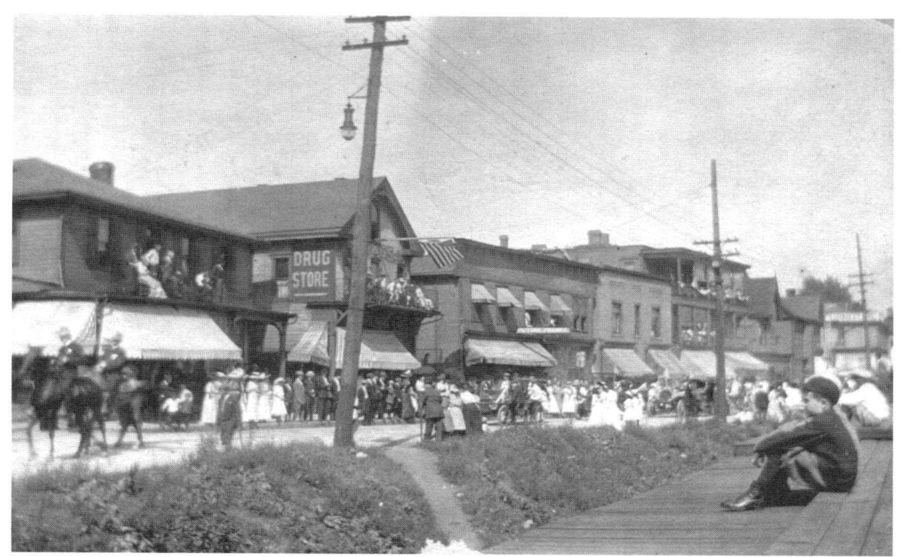

Boy watching parade down Sixth Ave. at Dickey Street, Tarentum (1921)

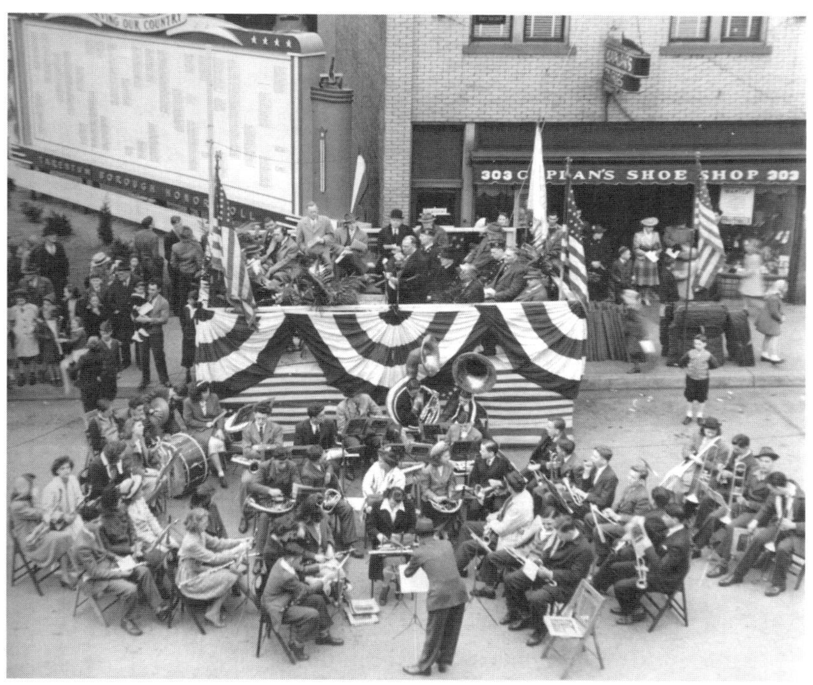

Band plays in front of Tarentum's WW II Honor Roll (1946)

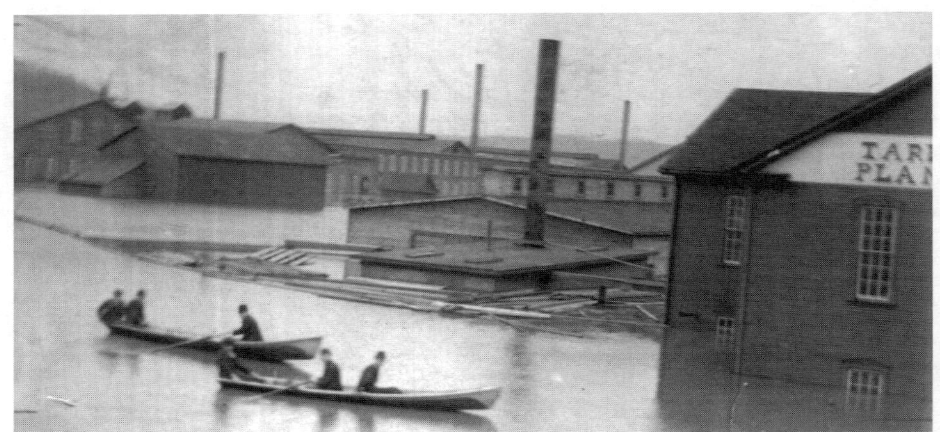

Flood at Pittsburgh Plate Glass plant, Tarentum (1891)

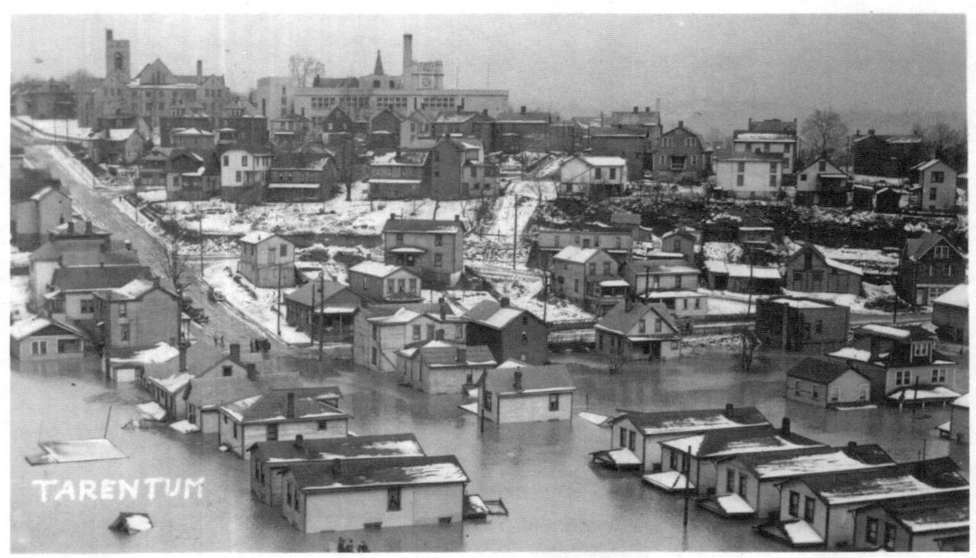

Flood in town of Tarentum (1936)

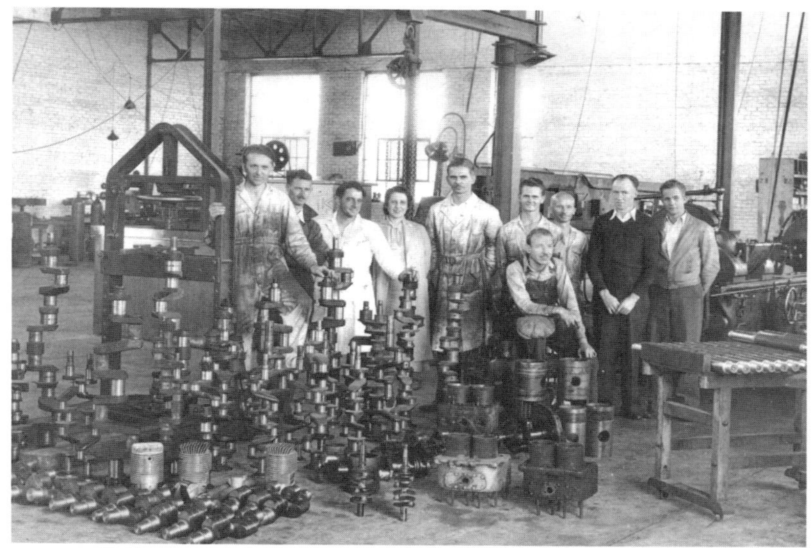

Engine repair shop, Tarentum, (c. 1930's)

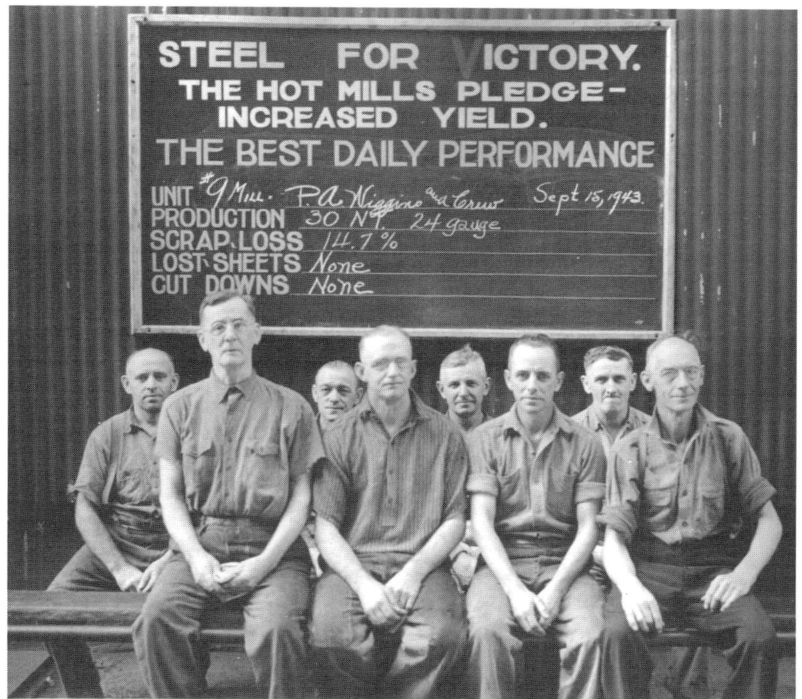

Hotmill workers from Allegheny Ludlum plant in Brackenridge, PA (1943)

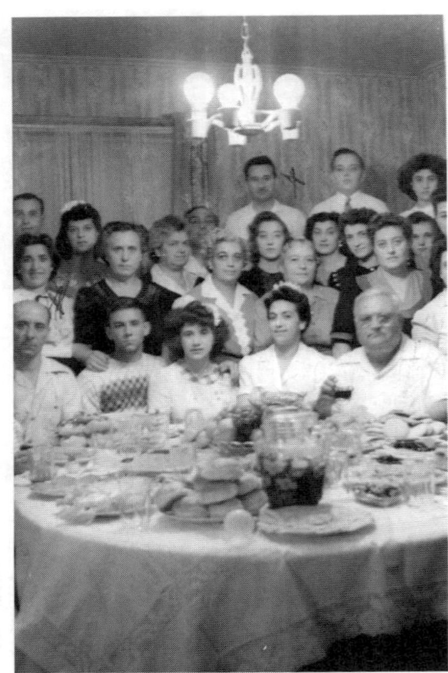

Going away party for Uncle Joe before he went to war in 1943; first row from right: great grandfather Anthony Geraci, grandmother Carmella, mother Vinnie, Uncle Joe, and grandfather Anthony Calderone

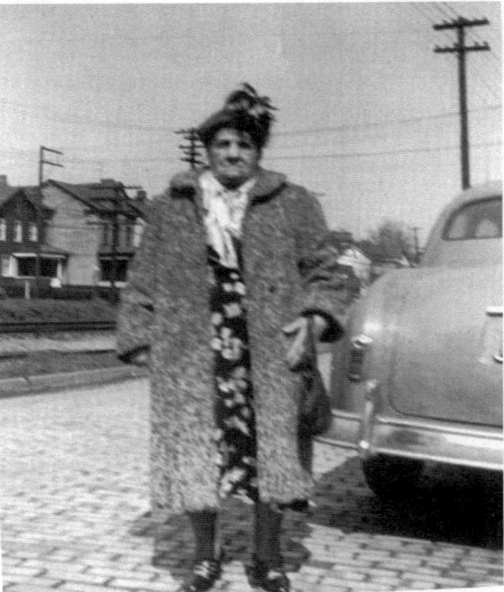

Great grandmother Filippa Scalia Geraci outside home in Tarentum (c. 1940's)

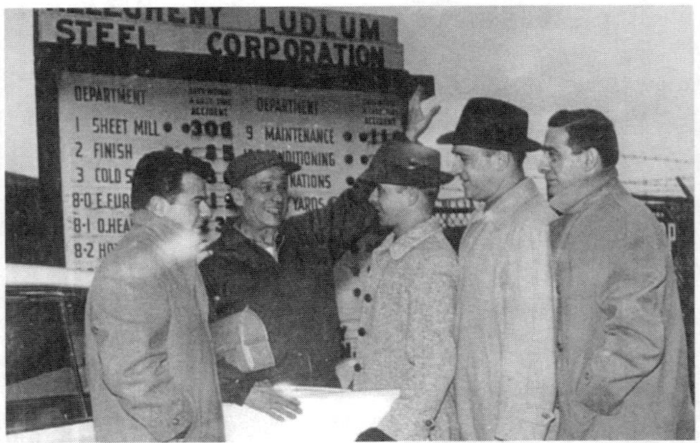

Grandfather Anthony Corso on last day of work as crane operator at Allegheny Ludlum; Uncle Frank, Grandpap Anthony, father Mario, and uncles Dominic and Angelo in 1960

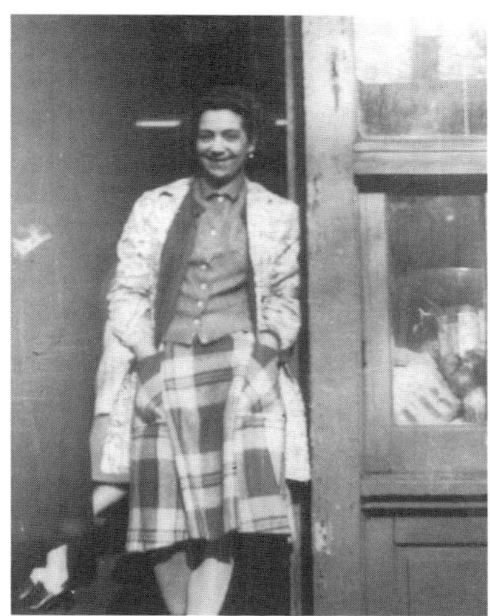

Grandmother Carmella "Nellie" Geraci Calderone before DiGirolamo's Fruit Market where she worked for 60 years. (c. 1940's)

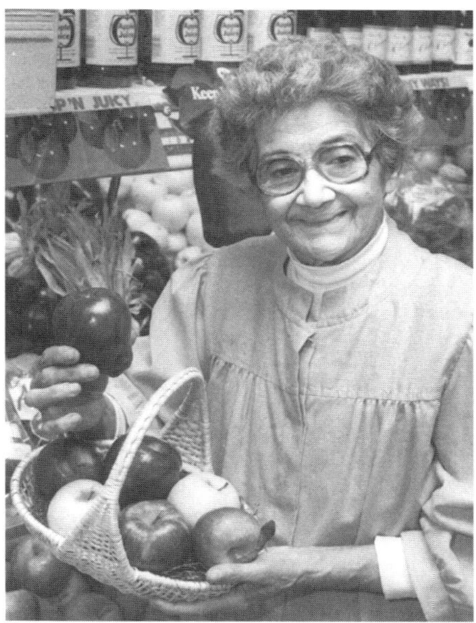

Nellie Calderone in fruit market, 1983; photo by Syl Zembrzuski for *Valley News Dispatch*

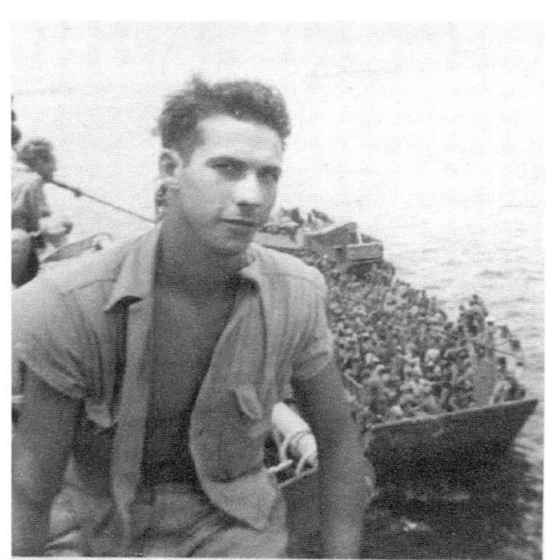

Father as young man before he went to college on the GI Bill (c. 1940s)

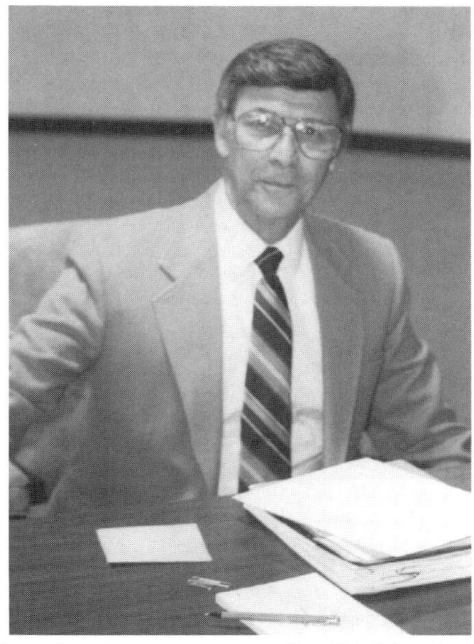

Father, business manager for Highlands and Chartiers Valley Schools, 25 years (c.1970s)

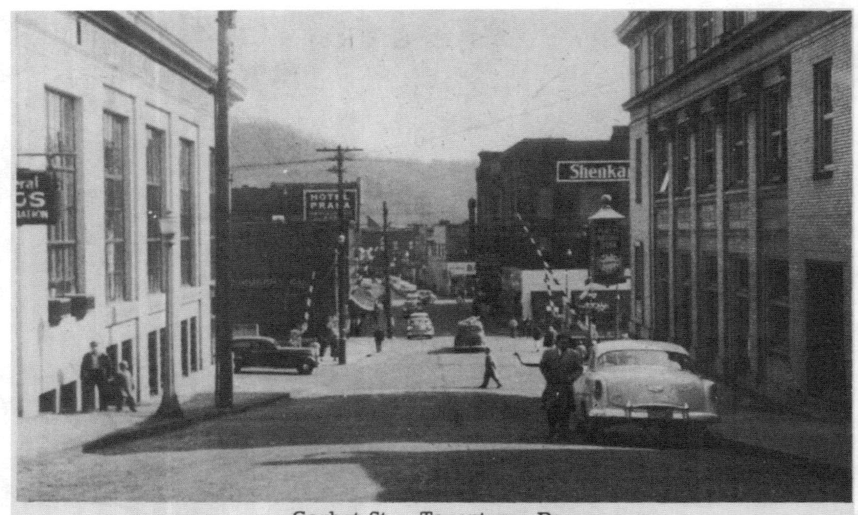

Postcard of Corbet Street, Tarentum (c.1950's): Murphy's, Kennerdale's Jewelry, Tritsch's Shoes, Praha Hotel; E.A. Lewis Ladies & Children's Wear, Central Drug, Book's Shoes, Tarentum Hardware, Confectionery, Shenkan Furniture Store

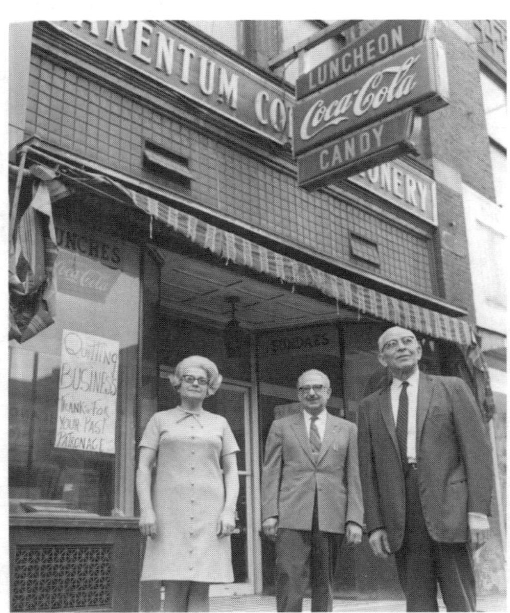

Tarentum Confectionery closes in 1971. Pictured are Aunt Mary Cieslinski (who worked there for 36 years) with co-owners George Papas and Philip Claditis; photo by William T. Larkin, *Valley News Dispatch*

STEEL PAPER CHIP

1.
bell-mouthed river
in nocturnal umber
sideswipes the queasy midland
jumpy from the rasp
of automation

industrialist smokestacks
his stainless wares
in a sky fortified
by fits and bursts
filling the hand
with shoveled heaps
of take-home pay

2.
sink-toothed laborer
in a disposable wrap
bandages her negotiated paunch
flattened from the wear
of indigestion

acid bites swallowed
with a noontime whistle
blowing more than
a worker can stomach
insides dissolved
steel into paper
paper into tumorous chip

3.
loose-lipped wizard
in virtual command

fast talks a white rabbit
accessed from his black hole
of information

ideas multiply
as their numbers dwindle
aging faster than
a caught fish thrown
back into the river
riding, disappearing, ridden

MADE OF STEEL *

My hand won't corrode if you hold it in the acid rain;
my lips won't twitter should you kiss them with island breath.

I will not billet or bloom though ambient temps quicken me
to roll and when a skimmed, bituminous gaze surfaces,

my eyes are rivets attached to the idea of combustion:
smelter my geology with your geography and wait for a reaction.

My face is disfigured beyond recognition yet it is not
foreign; my extremities are steel branches crooking past revision

so know that just because my ancestry is pig iron doesn't mean
I'm dirty. I am refined. I am refined.

I was once scrap but now I'm found, slabbed and coiled,
shipped and railed to a spacious morning near you. Leaving

little oxygen for me. Blow winds, blow, in steely voices
that scratch but always pardon a metal so base. A metal removed:

tapping, tapping, stirred; stirring, stirring then stored
and expelled, left for naught until soup kitchen ladies

pack me a steel brown bag with a handful of steel peas,
morsels of cold scrap that won't get lodged between my teeth.

While waiting, I file my nails with an emery board
(the edge of a truss bridge will do), and think if only

the line of those before and after me were a hot roll and our steps
overlapped, molten again, forming new ones with others to follow.

[*Title refers to mill Hunk legend, Joe Magarac, who was born in an iron ore mine.
Made of steel, he had arms the size of smokestacks and he combed his hands through
molten steel in order to make rails. He worked 24 hours a day and didn't have time for a
wife. When his true love ran off with another man, he went back to his beloved mill and
worked so hard that he made too many rails and forced the mill to shut down. He
threw himself into the fire at the thought of not being able to work.]

RIVER CROSSING

I.
Stronghold of mill Hunk
of hard hat and shovel
muscling water's edge
pockets of flexed gray
shift with union 8 to 4

II.
Warm from sacrifice
from gutted insides
of fire-eating ingot
offered at holy altar
to blood-thickening shallow

III.
Pierced by heavy noise
by spiral breaking surface
like one last gloaming stone
spinning reckless, sinking bottom
as fish float downstream

IV.
Stuck in mud
in stagnant breaths of clay
masking alluvial bottom
from harbored stillness
set in bone

V.
Jostled out of somnolence
out of long closing breeze
awakened to smothering dream
hot clouds and fast rain
without subtlety of womb

VI.
Teeming with motor boats
with engines chop-shopping waves
to boardwalk gamblers placing
lanterned bets with hands
patted dry on paper money

VII.
Peeling off another ocean
another sea growing younger
a lake not yet born
fishing for a conceivable pool
to die again unknowing

TAKING TURNS

                                Stop
          before you keep going around
     to know dizzy. Hair covers your eyes
     in the spin. Ears hear the whir   but miss

          the buzzer, the honk, the beeper, the bleep,
               bells on the sheep in the middle

                    of the living room floor. There you go again:

back, back too far.

FOR ONE WHO LEAVES

Your milk lily mind
leaves to study ivy
climbing up brick
the way it does here
on our vacant garage
or to send down
a basket of your A's
as if we could fry them like eggs
eat them for breakfast
to protein our day

The letters home
on daisy ass stationery
signed with curly initials
as bouncy as your hair
a nickname dorm girls give you
to white out who you stuck-up are
as if you can make that disappear
with the tip of an eraser
you never had to use before
but press 'til it bleeds

A college degree
four years to find a boy to screw
or a papery reason
to wear fleshy nylons
in some overheated city bus
to some elevator building
just to snag them on a metal desk
with no pictures of us or here
between the distance
of your invoiceable blotter

MOTHERLAND SKIN

Famished and fair
veins between moles
pockmarks like oval graves
dug for you who leave
reasons undeclared
except to fill your void moon
with the spring inside
another sky.
Bone knuckled over
zippered pinch of
metal teeth feeling
the way home
so you can scratch
at the fist of petals
that once blossomed
in your hands.
If you tiptoe
on her rock and clay
to let the river speak
she will tiptoe in your ear
but instead you wait
for the bank to shout back
your rambling fear
of a woman with only
a lead foot for an instrument
who cannot pause
one lotionless second
to unearth a crust
of porous lines you never
before shall breathe.

THE AERIALIST

The daughter I can't have taps nectar from the trumpet flower,

Wings beating above a patch of fuchsia. She migrates

In solitude with a haunting whistle for a song, the sound

Of wheels spinning. She feels attraction for crimson fingernails

So she leaves me and leaves me again for shades of red but always

Remembers that only a hummingbird can fly backwards,

Return to my waters to bathe. See herself the color of my sun.

PROXIMITY

1.
The river from a distance is not the same
        as the river up close.   In this dream

I find myself walking toward the bank
soupy with algae and slime but I dive
        straight over, my projectile suspended
in the mist until I reach a clear swirl of water,
        my arms an arrow spearing crystal that cracks
into a thousand pieces, each one a reflection
of me for when I don't want to see anything
        but my own vision of what is to be.

2.
The river up close is not the same
        as the river from a distance.   In this life

I find myself walking away from the bank,
clumps of leaves caught between my toes,
        the smell of fish and worm baiting my skin,
wetness hardening, settling into my joints
        so that every move dries stiff and brittle
enough to snap off a finger or toe, a limb
if I'm not careful as I crawl up the rocky bank
        that scrapes away edges of my life, pieces of dirt
rolling back into the river, into stillness earthed.
A current saved up, the pause of so many days
        waiting with abandon.

ELSEWHERE

If the town
will live
    (sidewalk
        footing merry)
whether or not
I live there

If I will die
    (grayful
        drag of concrete)
whether or not
the town dies
with me

If the building
will stand
    (bricks
        tilted skyward)
whether or not
I stand with it

If I will crumble
    (grounded
        pinch of mortar)
whether or not
the building crumbles
with me

If the river
will flow
    (ripples
        sending fluted)
whether or not
I flow with the river

If I will lie still
    (petrified
        flat of grain)
whether or not
the river lies
with me

Does this mean then
they are not dependent
    (feverish
        solder)
on me or I on them

Does this mean then
I will die
folded in my suitcase
in all my homeliness
    (lip
        of elsewhere)

RADIO LISTENER

driving old Route 28
the river at my side
like a close friend
in the passenger seat
who watches the road
as I scan the radio
in Mom's blue Regal
for a song that makes me feel
it's good to be home again
to hit every red light
through every town
just to stop and watch
as a watery sky
thickens with moonlight
a landscape to snap
into my own photography
a portrait where I always
sleep with moist hands
under the pillow and never
reach for a different sky

a commercial breaks

as I pull over
for Glen's custard
how creamy it still tastes
maybe because the owner
uses the same recipe
that's kept him in business
so he can afford to take
winter months off in Florida
while people in the valley
wait every spring
for the flavor to change

and I for another radio song
to sweeten my tongue
to keep from melting on

SECRETS

My sister is the one who told me about
the woods behind our childhood home,

the peach trees, lilac bushes and wild rhubarb
the old barn foundation where I played hopscotch,

the willow tree bull rope I used to swing on
to feel my menstrual pad rub against the knot,

the tree house to smoke cigarettes and play
strip poker, the place where I wasn't anybody's

daughter or virgin. I wasn't surprised by what
she said, having grown up in a town where

more members of my family worked themselves black
in the steel mill or glass plant or salt works than didn't.

The smokestack was our church steeple,
the haze rising in the sky our ascending angel.

She told me since they bulldozed the woods I'd be able to see
clear to the river if I could look out our old kitchen window,

a naked river once clothed in emerald green.
I shiver for it and I shiver for myself, for all the times

I was exposed in those woods, for the first time I was
wed in nakedness. With each chill I wish I could keep

thinking they were pure and so was I as long as my secret
remained hidden in the thicket's immaculateness.

How can I come home and walk behind the house
when my secret is bare and dirty, born from a bigger one.

How can I tell the new owners it was different
when they think of it as a toxic waste dump,

when they can look out the window to tender saplings,
to a wide river that sees beyond.

STROLLER RIDE

baby lids drooping

This is where Sam Houch lived. Well, how would you know? You haven't
  been home since you got pregnant. They found his father with his tongue hanging
    out, gassed during World War I. (could not speak, fuming) The house with the
      chipped yellow paint.

pastel puzzle

See the lady sitting on the porch step smoking a cigarette in her bathrobe.
  God knows you must be used to breathing a lot worse with all those taxicabs.
   A Marine lived there, Theodore Britt. He was the first in town to get killed
    in the invasion of Okinawa. (crackers where you positively aren't) I said
      smoking a cigarette.

fuzziness rising

Down the street from him was our high school math teacher. Everyone
  in class used to say she was masculine because she was strict. She had
   a handle on her purse but carried it under her arm. 'Least she carried one.
    (pocketbooked percussion, straps in minor) She's been dead for years
      now. The house that has the plaque over there on the corner. With the
        empty flowerbox.

square of air

Next to her was the Stokes family. I graduated with their son, Rich. He used to
  bring a lollipop for everyone in the class on Valentine's Day. (you are not licked)
   He's long gone too. The house with the laundry—even the clothesline rigged on
    the fire escape in your apartment faces back—for the life of me, who would hang
      sheets in the front yard.

fluttering souls

A seamstress lived on the corner. She was a dainty little woman. Ruth Kuhn.
 Very crafty. She was commissioned to do silkscreen blouses for Kaufmann's.
  (not wearing on me) You should have seen the work she did in those days—
   beautiful beadwork.

   bubbles bubbles

Let's cross the street. Derelicts set this place on fire. (do not burn sideways)
 They better tear down that filth before the roof collapses and kills somebody.
   Charred wood everywhere.

   fudgie smudgie

And you can't walk in the alley anymore either. I kid you not. (how to
 enter: front door ring, back door knock). The borough finally got rid of
  the dope heads and riffraff. Now this. Wait until summer when the kids
   play ball. I wouldn't dare let a grandchild of mine near that place. There's
    five pit bulls waiting to break loose behind that wooden fence. Hear 'em?

   boards that go arf

More business for the funeral parlor. Did you know they own a flower shop
 and a clothing store downstreet? And he's not even from here. Took over
  when Mr. Porter died. I told your sister and now I'm telling you. Don't you dare
   give him my business. (will, forgiven) Oh, and a print shop. For the holy cards
    when you're laid out in his coffin.

   open and close

SMOKING MIRROR

1.
I am the cold air
where they dammed
the bull creek
struck the oil cure
and salt of soda
where a tribe creased stone
spotted carpetweed
lurched, capitulated
to itch mites
but not centennial
noises to come,
a celebration of footing
in more than moccasins

2.
I am the cold air
where they chartered a road
to fleet-footed relics
surface mirrors framing
mirrors transparent mirrors
optical and automotive
no longer manufactured
though I scour the lot
for a silvered piece
of reflection pure enough
to see where I come from
and what is to remain
of the missing

DID YOU JUST PART THE WATER OR MY HAIR

I see a fish belly-up white
    riding the current
        or is it a barrette
    made of pearls

I see the tail of a silver serpent
    waving through the river
        or is it a strand of gray
    frizzy with discontent

I see a boat rising from the depths
    with many oars but no rowers
        or is it an ivory comb
    whose teeth arrange and smooth

I see you sitting on the bank without longing
    raising your hand to part the water
        or will desire touch me, divide me
    move the hair from my eyes

RIVER SEDUCTION

In seat-belt fastened departure
the altitude suits you,
all of you that I can see—
hips that meander through,
gentle curve of spine,
bosom rounded with song,
shoulders that glide
every inch of somewhere,
skin dimpled with ebb and flow,
long, streaming neck,
fleshy surface gaze
of a nude lying on a sofa,
posing for an artist's eye
brighter than the color of water.

For One Who Stays

if
the soul
of the town
were attached
to a string
would you
tie it
loosely
around your finger
so you
don't forget it
when you enter
dark places:
alleys
garages
church basements
to stack folding chairs
bank vaults
school stairwells
commerce chambers
to get a bucket of ice
stadium toilet stalls
casino coat checks
mega store fitting rooms
to try on
a pair of underpants
tastefully
over your own
or
would you
let it
kite the sky
with your winded breath
ticking above
puffs of dandelion

when you
choose to remember
it all depends
on you

A PROPER BURIAL

-for Nellie, Kayte, Philly, Vita, and Honey

Mrs. DiGi drags bushel baskets of potatoes, onions
across a sticky wooden floor out to the sidewalk,

green beans so crisp she might hear the raw snap
between her teeth. DiGirolamo's fruit store is open

for business once she and her sister finish buttoning
their corduroy smocks, pockets filled with pencils,

torn strips of wrapping paper to take phone orders,
knots of string, cherry pits from lunchtime—too busy

to sit down on the crate stools in the back room, standing
to eat eggplant with *sugo* on a thick slice of Italian bread

'cause it's better than steak and "nothin's too good for the poor,"
Mrs. DiGi says. She isn't much of a speller but she knows how

to price every fruit and vegetable in the store even when
pink grapefruits are nine for a dollar and "Mrs. B wants four,

so she does." She sculpts gift baskets, stacking and molding
pieces of fruit, figuring candies in the crack between

pomegranate and pear, bananas hugging navel oranges,
walnuts shimmering behind the cellophane wrapping.

Her sister hangs another customer picture postcard that smells
of anise from her fingers dunking biscotti in a *tazza* of coffee

while Mrs. DiGi cranks the awning to block the afternoon
sun like a pulled-down hoopskirt that lures passersby

to peek underneath. Before Mrs. B's husband
lost his job operating a crane at the steel mill,

the bells on their door rang more often than an altar boy's
during Mass. She calls to say she'll be late

to pick up her order since she's going to the beauty shop
to get her hair done but never shows again. Some permanent.

No more postcards in the mail from summer vacation spots;
Mrs. DiGi's sending her own instead—due bills to all the regulars.

When they quit coming back, store hours are shortened
then DiGi's closes for good. Mirrors hovering over empty

produce bins double the void except for brittle sprigs
of parsley, fruit stems that are umbilical cords lost

without their flesh. A ribbon of sun spools through the window
into open cooler doors. Rotting boards cover broken glass

like Band-Aids. To liven the street until a chain store levels
the block, the storefront is painted tasteful shades of green,

dressed up in funeral clothes before it's laid to rest.

PROMENADE

1.
Sucking on hard rock candy, just three pieces
from a quarter-pound bag tell time.
Watermelon-colored tongues spit seeds
at each other,
          a conversation

sown downstreet between the five 'n'dime
and bowling alley. The boys lead the way
to the record store.

             The girls follow
'cause there's only one way to go.

Robin tells Sally, Sally tells me, I tell Mary
with root-beer breath the name of the 45
inside Robin's bag. Mary answers back,
spraying my ear with sour apple dribble.
So candy wrappers are crinkled whispers,
padding my jacket pockets until the bulges
on my chest

          make me a woman.
2.
My daughter kicks a buckeye
no longer eyebright brown
or pocketed for good fortune,
its shriveled shell trips on
                cracks

in the sidewalk's concrete puzzle
along what was once Main Street
until her foot coaxes the nut
to roll again a sixth time
in less than a block.

She's counting.
We pass a storefront window displaying
tank-metal adding machines, the tape still
curled with numbers from my childhood.

A Coca-Cola machine rests on its rump,
red side, a broken bottle on the wooden floor.
She rubs her nose against the window
and asks what kind of store it was.
Office supplies, I say. Eager to round
the corner, she taps a buckeye
for the ninth time.

I am counting.

3.
I am floating beneath
the aluminum siding that covers a facade
with cherubs on the frieze work.
Air and light

seep through like dreams of the day
I jumped out of a stifling boxcar to follow
the railroad tracks here or the brisk
Italian mornings in the barn when I pulled
a sheepskin blanket over my head.

Wind or wrecking ball. I know
which deafens the pulsating quiet
of our main street, which will
demolish this building

sweetened by the dead.
I'll find another place to vanish
in swirling grains of wood,
tiny marble veins to escape
the particle board & Plexiglas chase
of a newly constructed Rite-Aid,

its aisle of remedies retreating,
its fortress wall expanding.

Why leave now

when I can watch my granddaughter
learn to walk, watch her reach
for a photograph of what
the town looked like, what I looked like,
what we together were.

THE STAR SYSTEM

Born again marquee
block lettering
bold facing
Bible tracing
Christian gospel
starring Jesus
every top-billing time

Boarded-up doors
posting no bills
rusted staples
on colored-paper corners
like drops of blood
dried to nail

Cracks in mosaic floor
sooted and sinned
though I wait for jujubes
milk-dudded manna
to drop from above
fill them in good 'n' plenty

Baby blue sweater draped
over ticket booth stool
mothering a litter
of stray kittens nestled
in Mary Magdalene folds

I touch the glass opening
remember a dollar bill
slipped through the slot
a ticket back with change
expect nothing in return now
just hungry feline tongues
licking fingertips dry

21ST CENTURY ARCHITECTS

Isaly's, once
(home of Klondike ice cream bars
thirty-two-cent "skyscraper" cones
waitresses in checkered uniforms & Keds)
will be the new 21st Century Architects office

       as soon as they rip out
(counters where men wearing tent hats & dirty aprons
shoveled trays of rice pudding topped with cherries)

(Formica tables we leaned over to eat
chipped ham sandwiches so fast the runny
barbecue sauce didn't get the bun soggy)

       as soon as they strip
(fans from the tin ceiling
with blades that sliced summer air
like lunch-bucket baloney)

(shiny chrome napkin holders old ladies used to apply
lipstick rather than walk all the way to the bathroom.)

       Instead they'll build
work cubicles, CAD stations and drafting tables,
a place they'll design a '50s-style diner opening
in the new mall to bring back   old times.

TRAIN SPOTTING

1.
My great grandmother lived a block
from the steel mill in a company row,
identical houses, yards, and views
of the railroad tracks across the street,

trains freighting slag and coke heaps
so often her dog, Elvis, didn't bother
to bark. Saturday nights my cousins
and I sat on her porch on two-legged

chairs, staring at yellow flypaper
that hung from the ceiling to see
if a bug dropped off from the train's
vibration, its rolled rattle orchestrating

operatic bellows inside telling us
my cousin was back from his pizza run.
Scuppi nuoi   my great grandmother
called out in Sicilian dialect, his nickname

as a boy for outgrowing shoes before
they got old. *Chistu caa*   Nonna's gums
clapped directions to get her false teeth
for chewing the thin, crusty squares.

She and her seven daughters gathered
around the dining room table, pitching
pennies into a pot for a game of Scat,
fanning themselves with their spread

of cards while Nonna cooled herself
with a rainbow of Italian silk
since she just went out. She asked
where was *beddu figlio?*   He's usually

here when the pizza arrives. Probably
on the other side of the tracks, waiting
for the train to pass. I stood behind Nonna,
braiding her long silver hair to a railroad

rhythm strand over strand. Later, Aunt Vita
played the piano until Lawrence Welk
blew bubbles on his TV show. I watched
one pop before floating off the screen

then waited for another caboose
to evaporate on the track so we'd hear
the Lennon Sisters singing again
as if nothing had passed us by.

2.
Without having to look both ways I walk
across the tracks. The warning gate points
toward a steaming sky fringed gray. How
rarely it drops, shrugs off the gravity

on its wasted arm to stop traffic. No cars
gunning across to beat it like my grandfather
did so many years ago to punch in at the mill
on time only his car stalled on the track's edge.

He left it there and walked. Minutes later,
a train nicked the front end. Now a car would
get stolen or ticketed first by a meter maid
who never makes her quota anyway.

3.
The caboose now a painted lady on the track,
lipstick red around mouthy windows open for business.
Hand the conductor your stub, sit yourself down

with stops along the tour for pics 'n' snacks,
microphoned wisecracks for remembering
acid whiffs of coke in swallowed perfume air.

YOU BIT DOWN HARD, YOU BROKE YOUR TEETH

Beneath the tar-bellied pothole is a street cobbled by wops on fours, kneeing brick by brick by brick, each shaped with the curve of a loaf of bread rising under hooves and boots and wooden wheels then flattened by a steamroller rolling-pin mama. Another era smoothed over with asphalt wonder. Another immigrant bubbling under the surface. Another generation never fed *pane* that wasn't made to be soft in the middle.

CORRECTIONS

In the flare of daylight
across spaded concrete
we step through barbed wire
they dare to scale
and a wall of engorged sweat
so cold and compact
it empties out our beginnings

In the flare of daylight
down triggered corridors
firing the smell of piss
we stalk those who took our place
sentenced to end overcrowding
to answer the $34 million call
if you build they will come
from out of state to double
the population of this dying town
960 more beds with warm bodies
blanket-tucked faces
that will never be mistaken for ours

In the flare of daylight
beneath the spiff of uniforms
the ghost walks
hoarding what we found
on these acres
of flax and wade,
                    escaping

FLOOD WALL

if they tame you

strip silver hues
jeweling your skin

feed you stones
    as skipping
        as fisted
            as gray

while they erect
a wall between us
to mortar your dreams

so I won't dream
        of you
      just rain
    in my pillow

with the promise
it all shall pass
through you
even the fever
that swells within

    then I will know

a river town
without its river

FOR ONE WHO STAYS

Your black Camaro
polished into superstition
by the lash of circular hand
wrapped in virgin cloth
ointments dip and groove
a vow never to show
your bounded reflection
or do you slip then vanish
in its cauldron of steel
fleck by bleeding fleck

The vespertine drives
running on sheenful rev
on smoke and noxious lies
to the milted waters
of his torn-dirty riverbed
with Greek Procrustean edges
that cut or stretch
the soul to fit
his tarnished instinct
you mistake for gold

Sporty bucket seats
a numbered stick between us
for shifting apart
or a space where our tossed wrappers
wouldn't touch if I took a ride
in your flat-tired fancy
junked or sold
in a six-mile radius
the voodoo nail spikes through
the limits of destination
all your headlights pretend to see

G: *With 40 selections, you'd think one'd be Frank Sinatra. How in the hell am I supposeta remember all 'is? Maria, get my bifocals on the buffet.* M: *Grandma, can't you see a flashing light?* G: *Yeah, two of 'em with my double vision. Over there on the buffet.* M: *I'll preset them for you so you don't have to dial. Here.* G: *Nobody answers.* M: *Listen before you hang up.* G: *How can I? There's no place to hang.* M: *She's at the window looking for the talk button!* A: *Hello!* G: *Oh, my garsh. Anna Marie, come on over.* A: Now what? G: *Do you want a maroon case? I said I'd get it for your birthday.* A: *You don't have to do 'at, Aunt Vin.* G: *Never you mind.* A: *You sound like Nonni.* G: *She woulda never had one of 'ese. She was too good at shoutin' across the yard. It was cheaper.* A: *No wonder she heard my dad, Mr. One Thousand Horns, with or withaht the winda open. Bet she coulda used one walking home from dahnstreet late at night after making baskets at the fruit store.* M: *Talk on your cell phones!* G: *She didn't walk home. The chief of police drove her and your aunt to the door.* A: *Then why monkey around with a pocketbook phone? That's what she'da called it, yunz know.* G: *Mine's heavy enough. I got my wallet, credit cards, keys, coupons, tissues, pills, a bag of gumdrops. Now 'is. And makeup, of course.* A: *I must be gettin' old, Aunt Vin. I like the same shade a' lipstick as Mom.* G: *Don't talk to me about gettin' old. My shoulder's sore from 'is. Designer doesn't mean lighter, you know.* A: *Everything in 'ere is e-ssential. 'Cept for the gum drops.* G: *You oughta try 'em instead of those gee-dee cigarettes.* A: *Don't worry 'baht me. Put rubbin' alcohol on your shoulder.* G: *I'm aht! Do you have some next door?* A: *Yeah, we got rubbin' alcohol.* G: *Bring it over after I take my bath.* A: *When would 'at be, Miss Jean Naté?* M: *Go home and call her.* G: *I'm not gonna take a phone in the tub with me.* A: *Then I'll flick the ahtside light like I always do.* M: *Call her!* A: *Jeez-oh-man, I will! Now how 'baht a knuckle sandwich, Madame Teach? And before I forget. I want a beige case for my cell phone.* M: *Why bother? You two never leave each other's sight.* G: *Beige!* A: *It's neutral. Goes with anything.* M: *Well? Are you going to call?* A: *Yeah, I'll call! But is she gonna answer?* G:

END PIECES

She sat her husband down
made the confession she stole food
from the refrigerator

You mean our refrigerator? You didn't steal nothin'.

Lou, I ate a sweet pickle and two slices of bread.
The end pieces.

That food's yours, Flo! I bought that for you to eat.

I didn't ask first.

You don't have to, for Chrissake. This is your home.

She opened the refrigerator
made herself an egg and fried Jumbo
He went next door to tell his sister

What does she know anymore, Lou?

Jesus Priest, she usedta grow her own cucumbers and can 'em. Put Heinz
to shame. And baked every week, too. Bread and somethin' sweet.

Forget about it. What's said is said.

Worked half her life at Liberty Mirror.
Brought home a steady paycheck and this is what it comes down to.
Over a goddamned pickle and two heels she hasta ask first!

Fran just told me there's gonna be more layoffs.
And the lucky ones who keep their jobs have to take pay cuts.
Do you think the big cheeses bothered to ask first? For somethin' like 'at!
That's more than a couple of heels and a sweet pickle out of the fridge.

He waved his hand in disgust
left for the Giant Eagle
Bought groceries for him and Flo

She was alone with four slices of bread
two sweet pickles, floating
in a jar of green juice and seeds.

EXHAUSTION

if she could use
her hands to fasten
a button twist a knob
scribble a letter
to tell me she dreams
about tailpipes
thirteen parts assembled
again and over
like a broken dance
of two palms
stroking rubbery backs
fingers bowing
to partners swollen
with gnarled collapse
snapping delicate cylinder
joints in place
for the socket and bend of it
as she dismantles her own
one occupation at a time
even before they tell her
with owning fists
to speed the quota
because flesh is thick
in a town that has no fire
just cold furnaces
and breadsinners
with lottery eyes or
bingo on their breath
so where can she go
if the work of her hands
is meant for reaching
the grasp of all things falling

Photographs of George Thomas Mendel

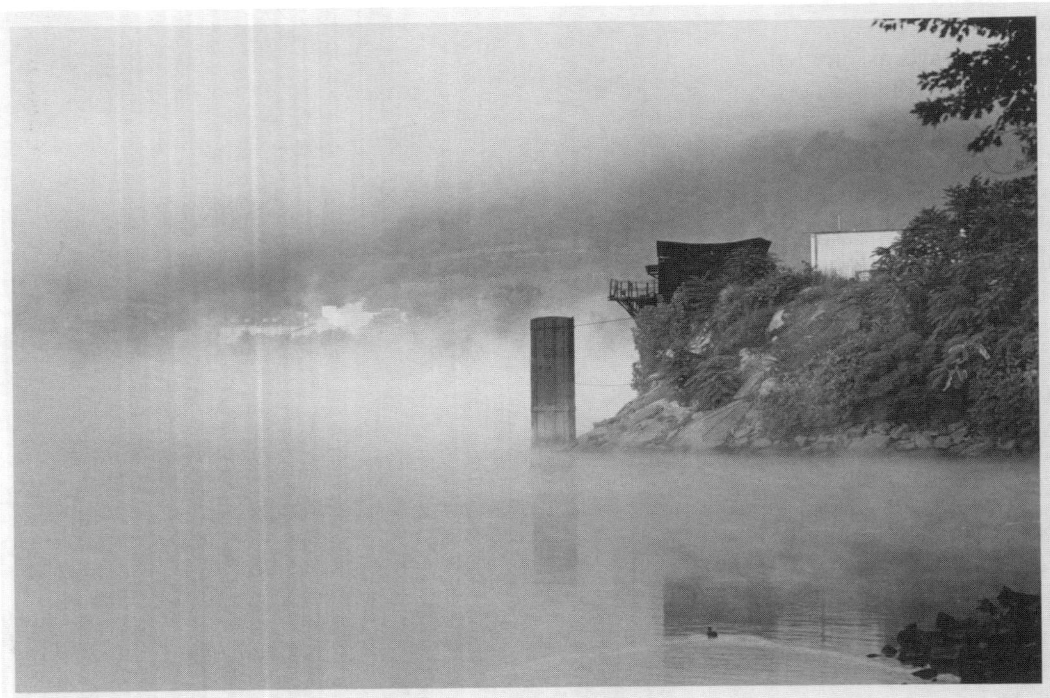

River Mist at Mooring, George Thomas Mendel

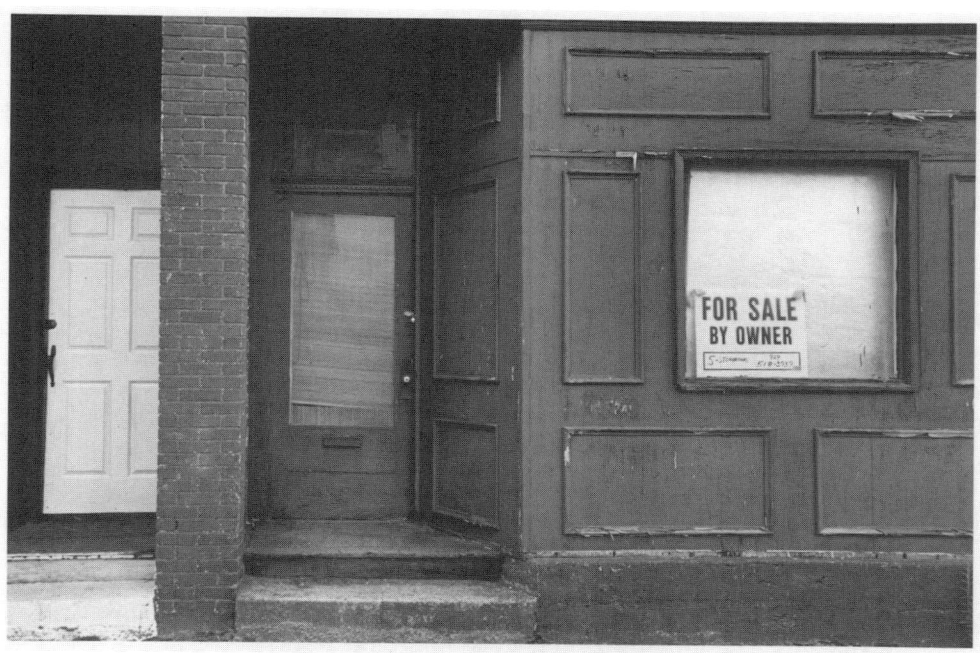

For Sale by Owner, George Thomas Mendel

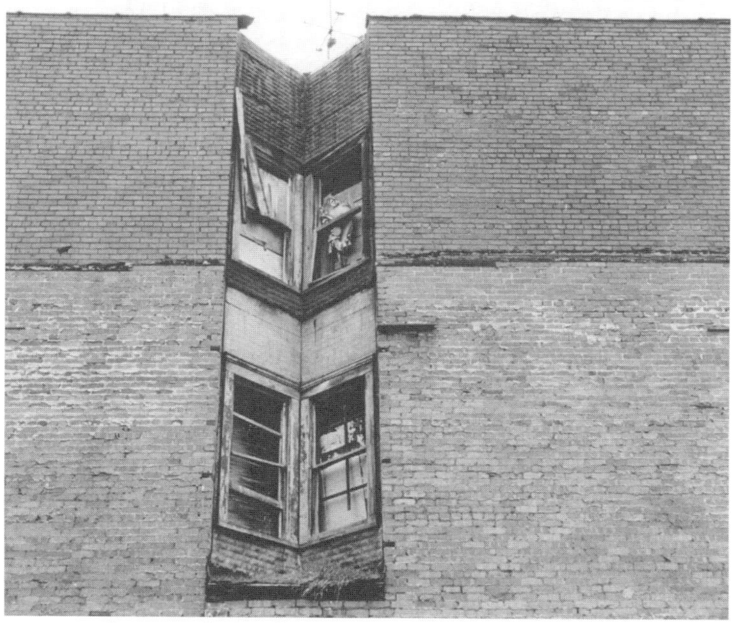

Recessed Windows, George Thomas Mendel

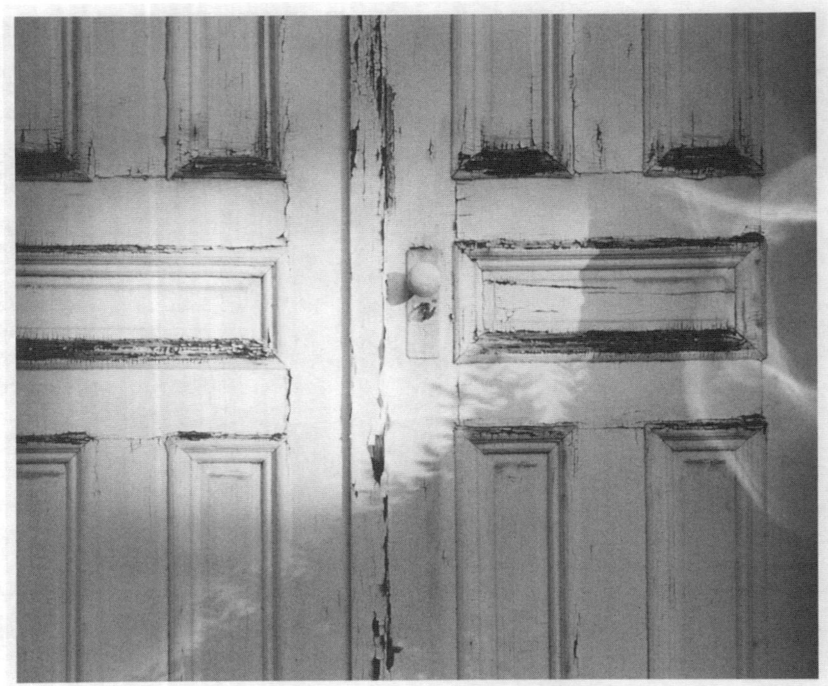

Church Doors, George Thomas Mendel

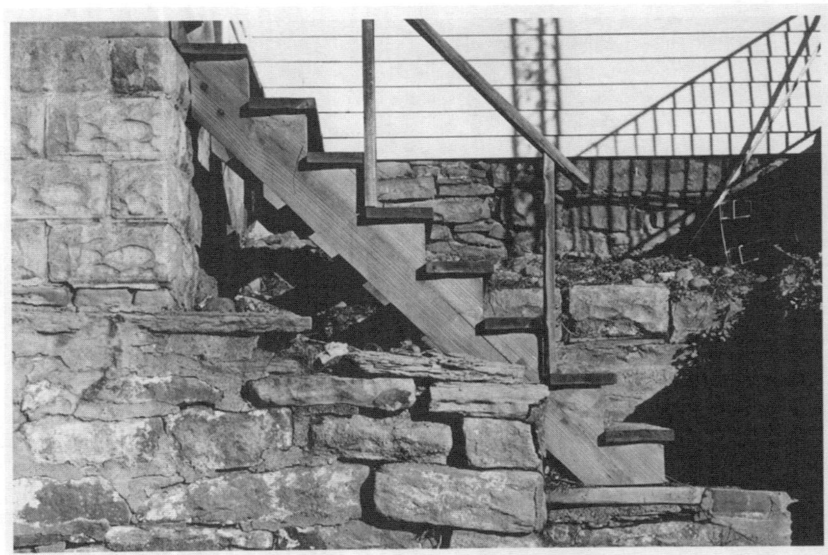

Replacement Steps, George Thomas Mendel

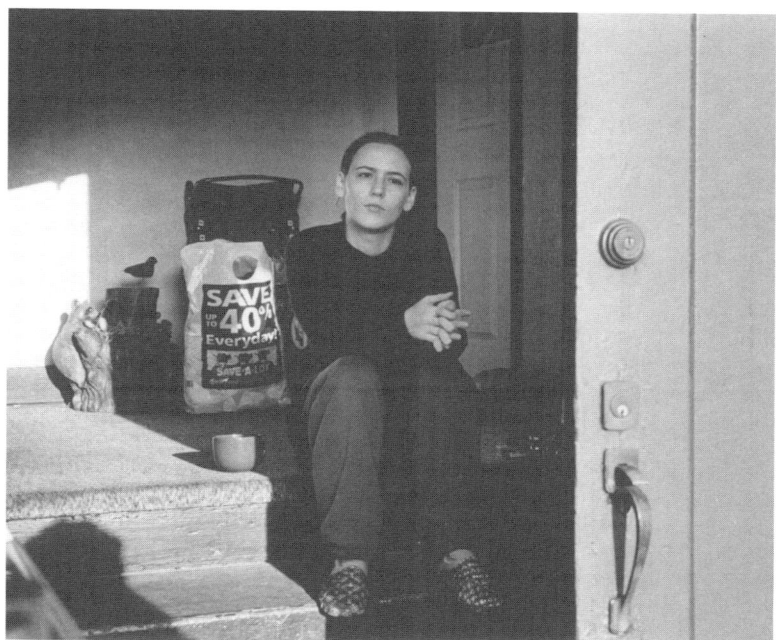

Save 40%, George Thomas Mendel

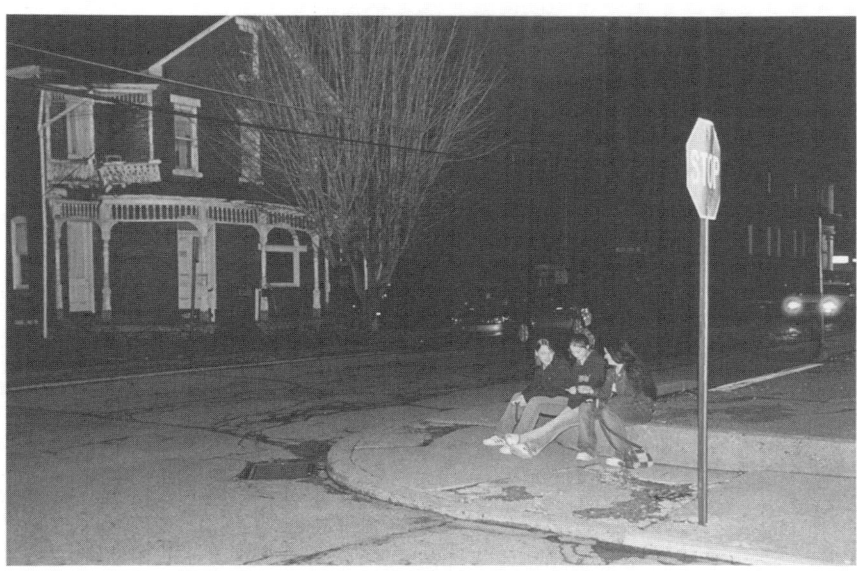

Street Corner Talk, George Thomas Mendel

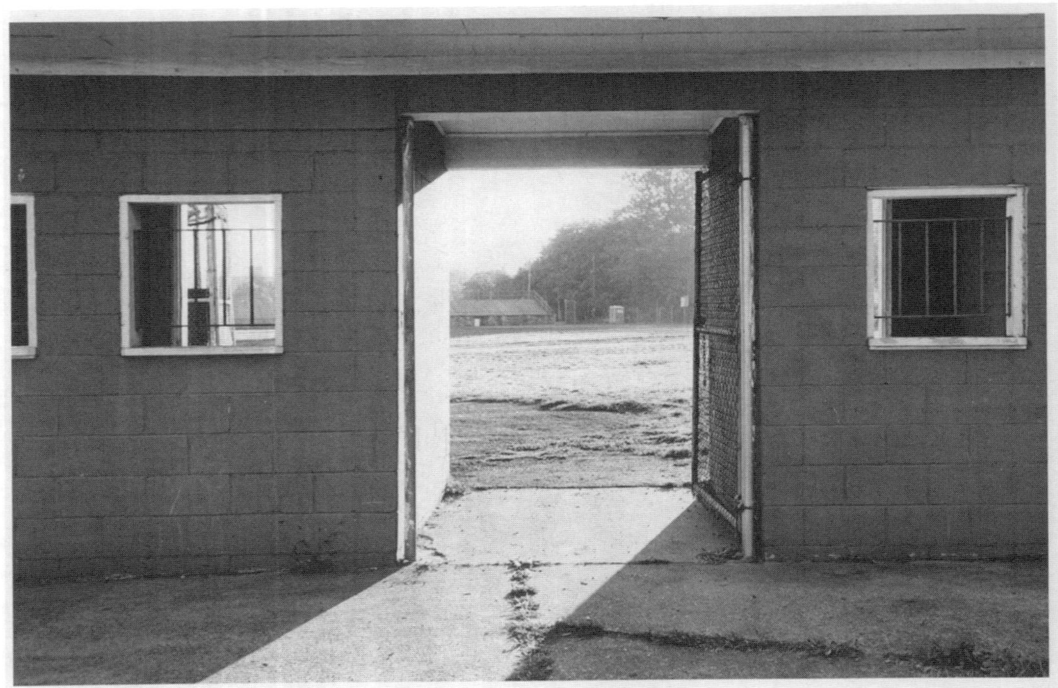

Ticket to Dreshar, George Thomas Mendel

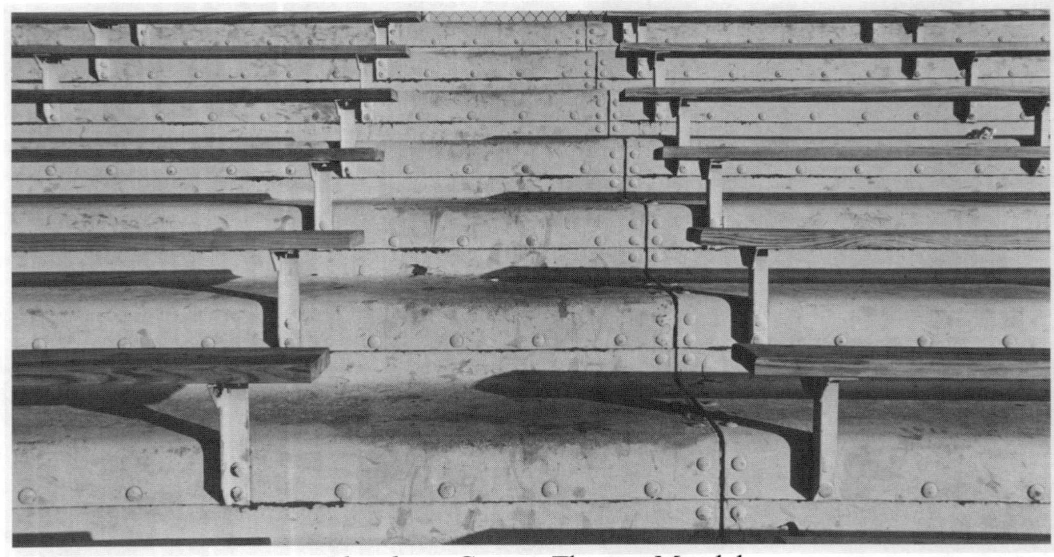

Bleachers, George Thomas Mendel

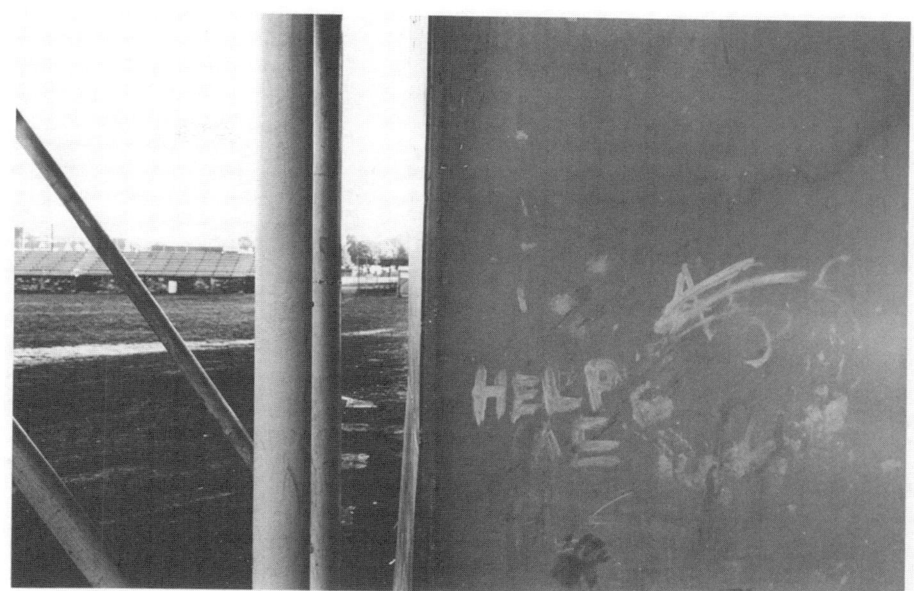

Help Me, George Thomas Mendel

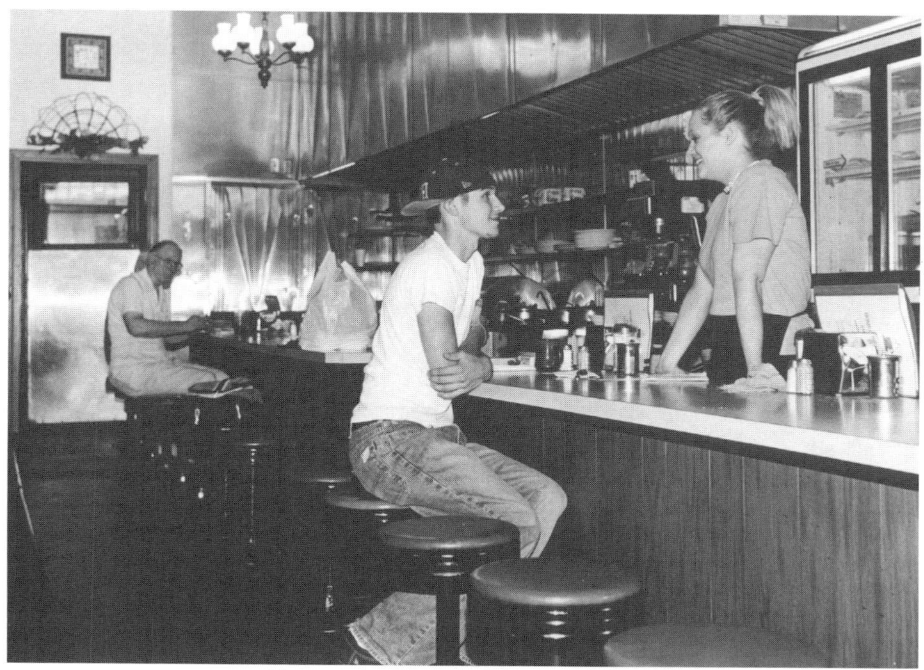

Massart's, George Thomas Mendel

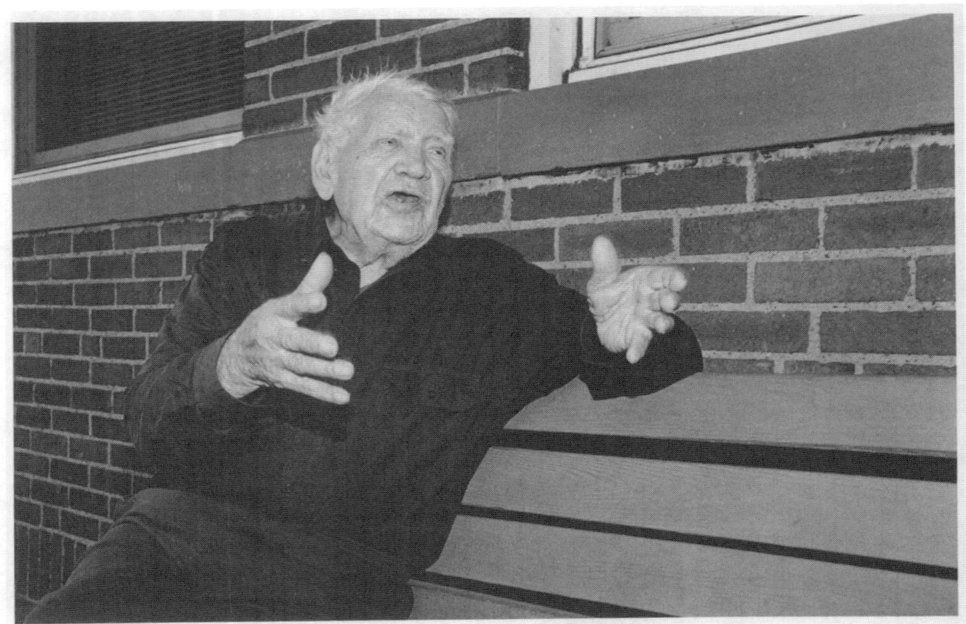

Master Glass Blower, George Thomas Mendel

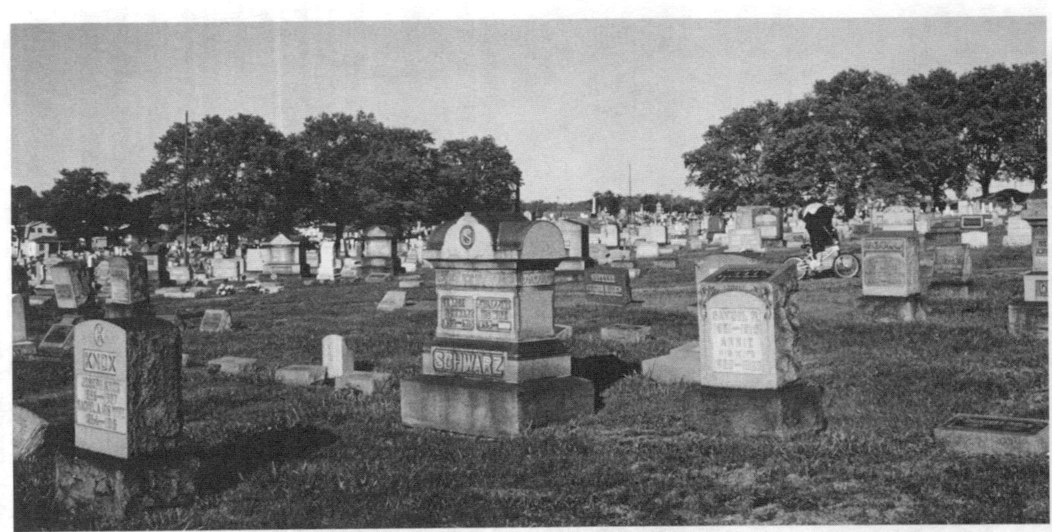

Short Cut, George Thomas Mendel

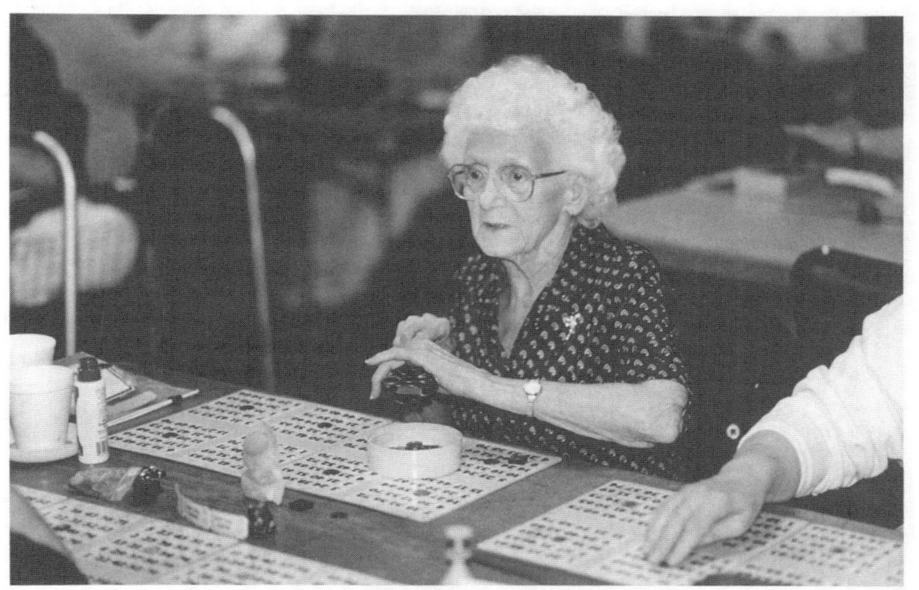

Magic Wand, George Thomas Mendel

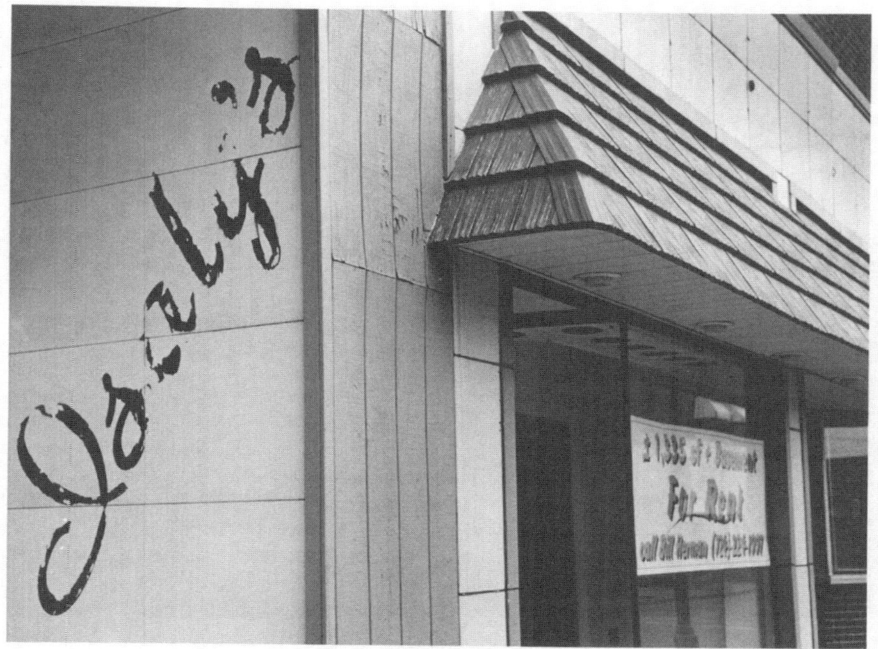

For Rent, George Thomas Mendel

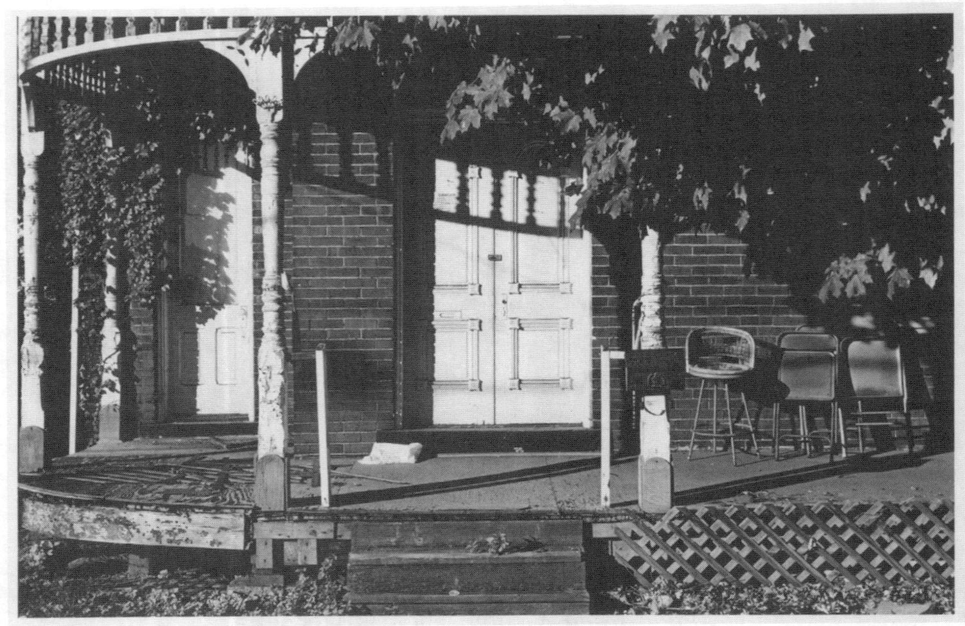

Wraparound Porch, George Thomas Mendel

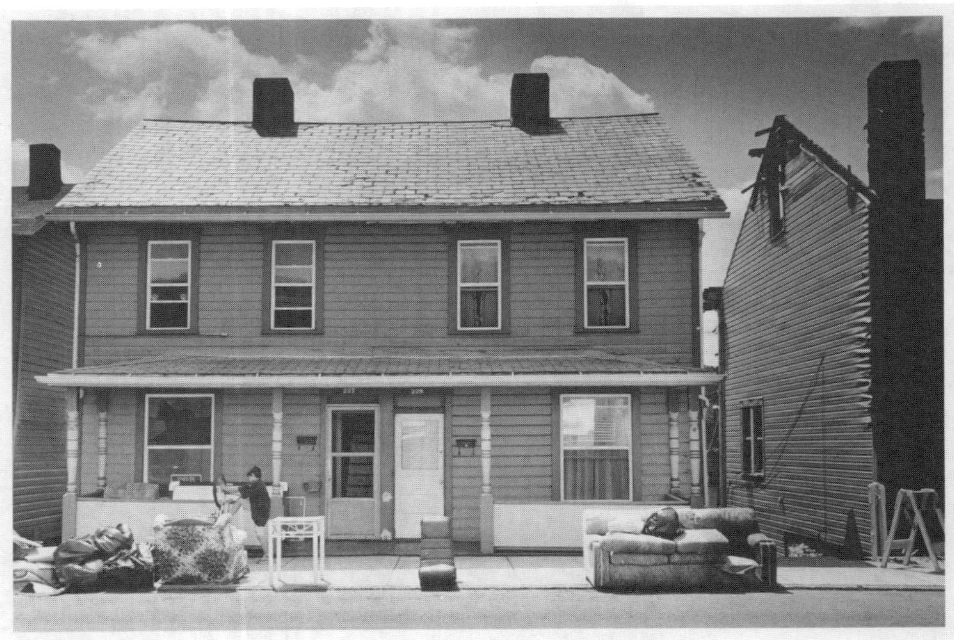

Bicycle Repair, George Thomas Mendel

River Crossing, George Thomas Mendel

THE RIVER INSIDE HER

There once was a river inside her,
     so she swam.
              She swam
and swam and floated
by a tender rock where boys
counted hobos on freight trains,
by a family pitching horseshoes
at a corn roast, drifting, drifting by
a woman sealing a jar of jam with wax.
She drifted farther still to a box of
checkers under a Christmas tree

until she could drift no more,
     so she paddled.
              She paddled
and paddled and kicked
beyond a blue island where
she remembered the day
a pilot and her plane disappeared
and a hero's baby was kidnapped

until she could kick no more,
     so she thrashed.
              She thrashed
and thrashed and bobbed
for air in a rapid current
where she grabbed onto tree branches
and shiny possessions with plugs
whose long electrical cords
reeled her into the riverbank

until she could bob no more,
     so she laid there.
              She laid there
and laid there and basked

in a sun so strong
it evaporated the river inside her,

until she could bask no more,
          so she prayed.
                    She prayed
and prayed and reflected
on her last breath of life
before they wheeled in a machine
with three images to resuscitate her.

When they pulled the lever,
a lemon, a banana, and a cherry appeared,
but she did not open her eyes.

When they pulled the lever again,
two lemons and a cherry appeared,
but she did not open her eyes.

When they pulled the lever once more,
three lemons appeared and she awoke,
inhaling and exhaling long enough to touch
the tender rock protruding from her bosom
then to roll over, leaving a puddle
left from the river inside her

until it too evaporated down to a drop
too small for even the wind to swallow.

A DRINK OF MAGNETIZED WATER

Sometimes

about to dare the open-wide roar
of the dam, the river's mouth
jeering spit that pricks her skin

she says to herself

inflated with orange push-me-up vest
with husky walkie-talkie and enough
muscle to rip stroke unopened water

I could stay on top

do more than bob my head
choke on water and pant for air
resist going down

underwater

under the covers to the bed at the bottom
to the underworld of sleep to what lies
under life, I could stay on top

if I had to

but she steps back from the ledge
dissects the water ripple by ripple
to find someone who thinks like her

She looks above and below the dam

spot boats filing into the lock
waiting for the gate to close
the water to rise or fall

like a bathtub civilization

a liquid empire filling up draining out
valves gripped hand over hand
with corresponding grind and chatter of teeth

around a circle of overbite

where the water level goes up
the water level goes down
in our cubicle of control

Sometimes

about to burn wetness that feels
the greater weight of a coin
forgets its name and moves in streams

she says to herself

tilting the ocular
congestion with dilation
flushing of face

a million ripples count them

each one a bump that falls flat
when the shivering stops
inhale and exhale paling color

green to scamper in a field

brown to print her feet on earth
gray to rub against stone
white to roll in sand

There in the vacancy

shadowing the lock so she can't see

anything as individual only as group
as mass of concave and convex

the river drips with sun's glaze

a million ripples count them as she shakes her head
waits for new thoughts to fall out and skip
into the river like stones skimming

a drink of magnetized water

Blow of gong
stroke of spine
vessels and spasm

metered ticking, soft, steady

a radio on low
whispering hum of breath
blowing in her ear

lightness of pause

a delicacy so rare
it could put a hypnotist
to sleep

a drink of magnetized water

Blow of gong
stroke of spine
vessels and spasm

metered ticking, soft, steady

a radio on low
whispering hum of breath
blowing in her ear

lightness of pause

a delicacy so rare
drops of water fall on her eyelids
water falls, her eyelids drop

a drink of magnetized water

Blow of gong
stroke of spine
vessels and spasm

metered ticking, soft, steady

a radio on low
whispering hum of breath
blowing in her ear

lightness of pause

a delicacy so rare
a hypnotist is asleep
sleep, eep, p.

RECESS

rocked and swaddled
her cove is brown
at the edge of green
mudbreath incubated
far away from current
rivering standby weather
alloys of reed stalk
accidental picnic
hushed downstream
to spear words unspoken
grilled on a stick
the wind is *pianissimo*
driftwood the moment
before rain
tips fingering
homesick raft
floating, consoling
easily deflatable
bedding stone
days shortened
by tennis-shoe kicks
by T-shirt skin
by heads bobbing
the eyeful water
light enough
to begin again

DEATH BY RENAISSANCE

Corso
is masculine
course
in Italian
the parade
in navigation
the way the path
the boulevard
in circulation so
I ask my father
the blood
of direction
he blushes, says
his mill town
needs a Boost
its count down
its economy
low on iron
scrap on platelets
far too long
his mill town
needs to eat again
a seven-course meal—
so what the courses
the course I ask
is the first
river gambling
diced roll
on "slag barge"
a claw emerges
from the water
with neon take
to wet a palate
appetize a pocket
bank it and lock it

is this the course
red cells
white cells
which will lead
the sanguine
gift of motion
the parade
in navigation
the way the path
the boulevard
in circulation
is the second
a juvenile prison
a pungent salad
of spears and spikes
of uncouth tykes
sleeping on cots
of wet dreams
and if life
is sentenced
in a handcuff
then job security
for guards and
makers of mush
to think crime
could be so flush
is this the course
which will lead
the sanguine
gift of motion
the boulevard
in circulation
is the third
a playing field
soupy with cleats
and turf enough
to artificial green
a commercial break
no matter

the win the lose
a well-endowed
sponsor weds
a wifely park
to take his name
and if seats
aren't filled
dump the broad
and marry again
in another state
willing to build
bags searched
at the gate
no food no drink
the price of a cheer
four for bottled water
and five for a beer
is this the course
the sanguine
gift of motion
the parade
in navigation
is the fourth
a strip mall
of chain stores
where the plant
once stood
a main dish
of dinosaur bones
dug under so
a new skeleton
gonna walk aroun'
CVS bone
connected to
Walgreen bone
Walgreen bone
connected to
Eckard bone
Eckard bone

connected to
Rite-Aid bone
worker hears
minimum-wage word
is this the course
the way the path
which will lead
the sanguine
gift of motion
is the fifth
tourism
a miracle
to touch
with a votive hand
a teary statue
a bleeding heart
a wallet stuffed
with steady pay
enough to feed
a family without
it having to
swallow creed
is this the course
red cells
white cells
in circulation
is there room
for dessert
or cheese
a sweet rushing
the stream
a Gorgonzola
hunk with prosciut'
to cholesterol
another
development
scheme
so I ask
my father

is a town
still alive
if its reason
for being
no longer exists
or is it just
a real estate
location or
money gyration
not home
but he's not
the one to say
no transfusion
no stranger's blood
his taste's metallic
skin singed
chemical warfare
a day of retreat
a walk along
the river past
the school
he dago flunked
until he learned
the speak
the steel mill
he operated
sweatbox crane
then war to gun
fighter plane
the university
to skin a degree
the river he left
to discover
his Italian name
only to find it
home again so
I ask my father
is his course
the town's

a life prolonged
if the blood
of direction
is moving still

Acknowledgments

Grateful acknowledgment is made to the editors of the following publications in which earlier versions of these poems appeared:

Connecticut Review: "Proximity"; *O Taste and See: Food Poems* (Bottom Dog Press): "End Pieces"; *Italian Americana*: "The Same Fish Twice" and "Author's Preface"; *Loyalhanna Review*: "Architects 2000"; *Many Mountains Moving*: "Exhaustion"; *New Delta Review*: "The Star System"; *Pavement Saw Magazine:* "Steel Paper Chip"; *Pittsburgh Post-Gazette*: "Allegheny River Seduction" and "21st Century Architects"; *Poet Lore*: "Promenade"; *Poetry in Performance*: "If"; *Poetry Motel*: "Smoking Mirror"; *Sudden Stories* (Mammoth Books): "The River Inside Her"; *The Progressive*: "Made of Steel"; *Western Pennsylvania History*: "Saturday Mornings," "My Very Own Cleaning Lady," "Expressed,"and "The Doctor Makes His Diagnosis"; *Women's Studies Quarterly*: "400 Tons or Twenty Five Thousand Dollars a Day."

The following poems appeared in the chapbook *A Proper Burial* (Pudding House, January 2003): "River Crossing," "End Pieces," "Exhaustion," "Call Girls," "Promenade," "21st Century Architects," "Train Spotting," "Corrections," "A Proper Burial," "Radio Listener," and "Flood Wall."

Thanks to S. Hartley Johnston and Cathy Wencel of the Allegheny-Kiski Valley Historical Society, the Community Library of Allegheny Valley in Tarentum, and Brian Butko at the Heinz Pittsburgh Regional History Center for their research support; to my mother Vinnie, my sister Mary Ann, the Joseph Calderone family, Mary and Antoinette Cieslinski, Mary Ann Geraci, and my father's brothers and sisters, Angelo, Antoinette, Dominic, Frank, and Grace for passing on their stories and sharing family photos, to the *Valley News Dispatch* for staff photos, and finally to photographer George Thomas Mendel.

Sincere gratitude to my teacher Felicia Bonaparte at the City College of New York, Julia Cole, Jim Daniels, Elizabeth Frost, Nandita Ghosh, Edvige Giunta, Scott Hightower, Sybil Kollar, James Lui, William Mack, Evan Marshall, Mary Speaker, Judith Vollmer, Christopher Winks, Michael Wurster, and Janet Zandy for their generous comments and support. I would also like to express my appreciation to the New York Foundation for the Arts for awarding me a poetry fellowship.

Special thanks to my husband Michael Winks.

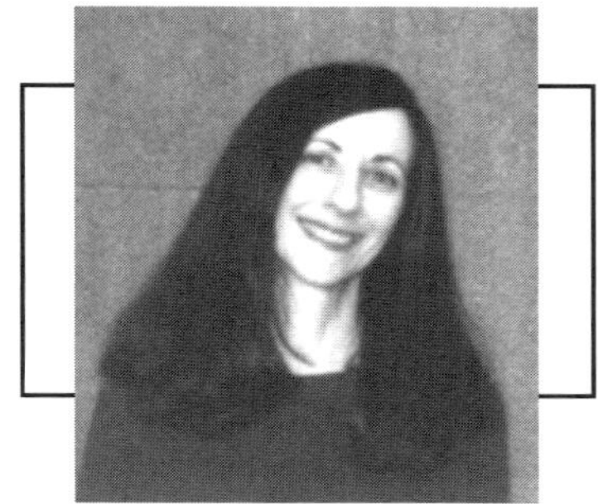

Paola Corso

Paola Corso was born in a Pittsburgh river town where her Italian immigrant father and grandfather worked in the steel mill. She earned a B.A. from Boston College and a master's degree from the City College of New York-CUNY where she won the Dejur Award for Creative Writing. She is a 2003 New York Foundation for the Arts poetry fellow, the 2003 Bordighera Poetry Prize First Runner-Up chosen by Donna Masini, and author of the Pudding House chapbook *A Proper Burial.* Her poems have appeared in *Italian Americana, The Progressive, The Pittsburgh Post-Gazette, Western Pennsylvania History, Women's Studies Quarterly, New Delta Review,* and elsewhere. She currently teaches a creative writing workshop at Fordham University and lives in Brooklyn with playwright Michael Winks and son Giona.

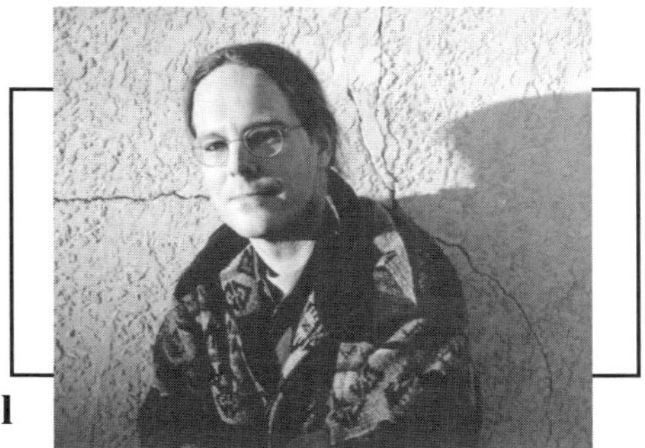

George Thomas Mendel

Photo by Bambi Cantrell

George Thomas Mendel, a photojournalist and fine art photographer for more than 20 years, has published in numerous books and magazines and has produced a variety of portfolios, including architecture and humanitarian projects. Many of his fine art pieces have been auctioned for charity or donated to non-profits. These projects and his commercial endeavors can be viewed on the web at www.photo-now.com.

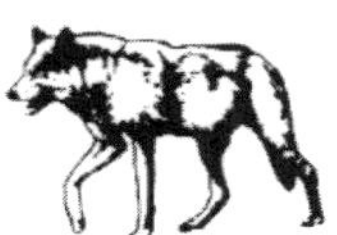